Essential Histories

The French-Indian War
1754–1760

Essential Histories

The French-Indian War
1754–1760

Daniel Marston

First published in Great Britain in 2002 by Osprey Publishing,
Midland House, West Way, Botley, Oxford OX2 0PH, UK
443 Park Avenue South, New York, NY 10016, USA
Email: info@ospreypublishing.com

CIP Data for this publication is available from the British Library

ISBN 978 1 84176 456 6

Typeset in Monotype Gill Sans and ITC Stone Serif
Editor: Sally Rawlings
Design: Ken Vail Graphic Design, Cambridge, UK
Cartography by The Map Studio
Index by Alison Worthington
Picture research by Image Select International
Originated by PPS Grasmere Ltd., Leeds, UK
Printed and bound in China through Bookbuilders

09 10 11 12 13   16 15 14 13 12 11 10 9 8 7

For a complete list of titles available from Osprey Publishing
please contact:

NORTH AMERICA
Osprey Direct, C/o Random House Distribution Center,
400 Hahn Road, Westminster, MD 21157
Email: uscustomerservice@ospreypublishing.com

ALL OTHER REGIONS
Osprey Direct, The Book Service Ltd, Distribution Centre,
Colchester Road, Frating Green, Colchester, Essex, CO7 7DW
E-mail: customerservice@ospreypublishing.com

www.ospreypublishing.com

Dedication

To Nancy

Contents

Introduction

The French-Indian War is the name commonly given to the conflict which arose in North America in 1754–55, between the British Thirteen Colonies (and Nova Scotia) and New France (comprising Louisiana, the Ohio River Valley, Quebec [known as Canada], and Cape Breton and St. Jean Islands). Following the War of the Austrian Succession, which was officially concluded by the Treaty of Aix-la-Chapelle, Great Britain and France continued their disputes over land boundaries in North America. The fighting chiefly took place along the frontier regions of the northern Thirteen Colonies and in the Quebec and Cape Breton regions of New France. New France was at a numerical disadvantage due to a disparity in population:

New France had 75,000 settlers, while the Thirteen Colonies had 1.5 million people.

The frontier skirmishes of 1754 propelled both France and Great Britain to seek Continental allies. With Europe firmly divided into two camps – France, Austria and Russia on one side and Prussia and Great Britain on the other – conflict was inevitable. By 1756, the frontier skirmishes had developed into a fully-fledged war in North America and spilled over into conflict in Europe itself. While it was connected to the larger, worldwide campaign known as the Seven Years' War, the French-Indian War anticipated that conflict by a year and served as one of the spurs to the eventual outbreak of hostilities in Europe and on the Indian

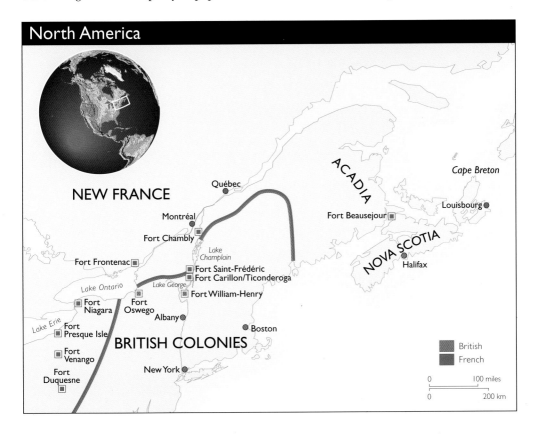

North America

George II, King of Great Britain. (Ann Ronan Picture Library)

subcontinent. (For more detail on the war in the rest of the world, please see the Essential Histories *The Seven Years' War*.)

The French-Indian War was fought in the forests, open plains, and forts of the North American frontier. The French Army, supported by allied Indian tribes and local colonial forces, initially benefited from a superior understanding of how to operate in the forests of North America, although throughout the conflict it was numerically inferior to the British Army. The British Army was also bolstered by colonial forces and allied Indian tribes, but in the early days of the war suffered from lack of experience and tactical knowledge of fighting in forest terrain. The British learned the lessons of their early defeats, however, and their subsequent tactical and training reforms ultimately enabled them to outperform French forces, both in skirmishes in the forests of the frontier and in continental-style battles at Louisbourg and Quebec.

Great Britain was to emerge from the French-Indian War as the dominant European power on the eastern seaboard of North America. As with the War of Austrian

Louis XV, King of France. (Ann Ronan Picture Library)

Succession, however, the French-Indian War did not signal the end of conflict in the region. Within 13 years of its conclusion, Great Britain was at war with the colonists she had sought to protect in North America.

The war strained relations between the mother country and her colonial subjects. France, seeking to reverse the misfortunes of the French-Indian War, was only too happy to undermine British superiority in the region, and threw her support behind the fledgling United States in 1778.

Chronology

1754   **27 March** Skirmish at Great Meadows
       3 July Battle at Fort Necessity

1755   **June** British siege and capture of
Fort Beausejour
6–9 July Braddock's Defeat
17 August British force arrives
at Oswego
8 September Battle of Lake George

1756   **17 May** Formal Declaration of War
between France and Britain
14 August British Fort Ontario, Fort
Pepperell, and Fort George at Oswego
capitulate

1757   **9 August** British Fort William
Henry capitulates

1758   **8 July** Battle at Fort Carillon
(Ticonderoga)
1 August French port of Louisbourg
capitulates
27 August French Fort Frontenac is
sacked
14 September Grant's Battle outside
Fort Duquesne
12 October French repelled at
Fort Ligonier
24 November French Fort Duquesne
is abandoned

1759   **24 July** Battle of La Belle Famille
26 July French Fort Niagara
capitulates

26 July French Fort Carillon is
abandoned
31 July French Fort St. Frederic
(Crown Point) is abandoned
31 July British attack on
Montmorency Falls
August Countryside around Quebec
laid waste by British forces
13 September First battle of the
Plains of Abraham
17 September Surrender of Quebec

1760   **28 April** Second battle of the Plains
of Abraham (Sainte-Foy)
Early September Montreal
surrounded by three British columns
8/9 September Montreal surrenders

1761–62 War continues in the Caribbean,
India, and Europe

1763   **10 February** Treaty of Paris
15 February Treaty of Hubertusburg
10 May–15 October Indian siege of
Fort Detroit
End of June All British forts in the
west captured except for Forts Detroit,
Niagara, and Pitt
31 July Battle of Bloody Run
5/6 August Battle of Bushy Run
10 August Fort Pitt relieved by
British forces.
7 October Royal Proclamation of 1763

1764   **December** End of the Indian Uprising

Tension in the Ohio River valley

The conflict in North America had its formal beginnings in 1754. Following the end of the War of the Austrian Succession (1740–48), French and British colonists, motivated by desire to expand their domains into the rich Ohio River valley, edged closer to armed conflict. The area along the Ohio River was considered to be uncharted, and thus formally unclaimed by either side. The British contended that the area should be open to both sides for trade, and followed this claim with the establishment of the Ohio Company. The French, however, viewed this as a British attempt to claim the entire area, and responded by sending both militia and regular troops into the region to build forts and eject any British settlers or traders found there.

Tensions had also risen in Acadian Nova Scotia, particularly along the Bay of Fundy. The French had established several new forts whose locations the British colonial governments considered to be in violation of the Treaty of Aix-la-Chapelle (1748). Both sides claimed large areas of present day New Brunswick, and considered the other the transgressor. The insult offered by these encroachments was compounded by the French government's relations with the Acadians, a French-speaking population who, as a result of treaty agreements, had become subjects of the British Crown. The French authorities deliberately stirred the Acadians' aspirations to independence, incensing the British governors. The establishment of Fort Beausejour in the disputed area was the last straw, as this made it apparent to the British colonists that the French had them surrounded. They were not being paranoid; the French did in fact intend to construct a series of forts from Louisbourg to New Orleans, enclosing the British colonies. The

hostility between the two countries was near to breaking point.

Governor Robert Dinwiddie of Virginia decided to make a move against the French in the Ohio River valley, while Governor William Shirley of the Massachusetts Bay Colony was to organize a move against the French in the Bay of Fundy. (This second campaign will be discussed later, as it took place in 1755.)

The British had begun to build a fort at the forks of the Ohio River in 1754. A Virginia militia officer, Lieutenant Colonel George Washington, then 23 years old, was ordered to march into the Ohio River valley with 200 men, to assist with and protect the

George Washington as an officer in the Virginian Provincials. (Ann Ronan Picture Library)

fort's construction. Washington and his men left on 2 April. News arrived on 20 April that the French had already moved against the British at the forks of the Ohio and forced them from the area. The French seized the fort and renamed it Fort Duquesne, after the Governor of New France, Marquis Duquesne. After a council of war at Wills Creek, Washington decided to continue to move towards the region, after establishing Fort Cumberland at Wills Creek.

Various other colonies decided to send reinforcements to the region. A Regular Independent Company from South Carolina moved into Virginia. Militia troops from North Carolina marched north to provide support, while Pennsylvania decided to grant money towards the cost of the expedition. These were helpful gestures, but the reinforcements were small and inadequate to the task that they potentially faced: undertaking the defense of the frontier. Washington continued marching towards an enemy that vastly outnumbered him, when he should have remained at Wills Creek and waited for reinforcements.

On 7 May Washington and his small force reached Little Meadows. Ten days later, on 17 May, the force reached the Great Crossing of the Youghiogheny. By 24 May, Washington reached an area named Great Meadows where, after receiving intelligence that a party of French troops was moving against him, he began to build fortifications, naming the structure Fort Necessity. On 27 May, Washington and 40 militia soldiers moved 9 km (six miles) distant to ambush the French detachment. Washington hoped to surprise the French camp, but the alarm was sounded. The battle was short but brisk. The French commander, Ensign Coulon de Jumonville, was killed, along with nine French soldiers, and 21 French soldiers were taken prisoner. One French soldier escaped and reported back to Fort Duquesne. The Virginia troops lost one killed and three wounded. This skirmish signified the opening of armed hostilities.

Washington decided to remain in the area, to build up the defenses of the fort and

the road towards Fort Duquesne. On 9 June, a further reinforcement of 200 Virginia militiamen arrived, followed by reinforcements from the Independent Companies of South Carolina on 12 June. Welcome as fresh troops were, their arrival sparked an immediate tussle over the politics of command. The Independent Companies were on the British Establishment, which meant that their commander, Captain James MacKay, was senior to Washington. While MacKay did not attempt to assume command, he refused any orders from Washington for his men.

On 16 June, Washington moved out towards Fort Duquesne with his Virginia troops, while the Independent Companies remained at Fort Necessity. Reports from scouts claimed that the French garrison was reinforced by more than a thousand men, and that the Shawnee and Delaware Indians had sided with the French. Less than 32 km (20 miles) from Fort Duquesne, Washington stopped to hold a war council with the Delawares and Shawnees, hoping to convince them to switch their allegiance. On 28 June reports arrived that the French, with their Indian allies, were moving towards him.

The Independent Companies caught up with Washington on 29 June, and MacKay and Washington agreed to withdraw towards Wills Creek and then on to Fort Necessity. The withdrawal to Fort Necessity was hard going, due to the number of horses and wagons that had to be left behind. The exhausted troops arrived at Fort Necessity on 1 July and began to prepare the area for battle.

A French detachment of 500 soldiers and allied Indian warriors, led by Captain Coulon de Villiers, brother of Jumonville, marched on the heels of Washington's force. The French came upon the Great Meadows area on the morning of 3 July. Villiers decided to fan out his troops to draw fire and locate the enemy forces. The French and Indian forces immediately drew heavy fire, so Villiers kept the majority of his men in the forests to the west and south of the British positions. Villiers advanced cautiously as the British troops withdrew into the entrenchment surrounding the fort. The French and Indian troops fired into the British positions from the edge of the woods. The fighting lasted for nine hours, and the British suffered not only losses under fire but also from a considerable number of desertions. The rainy weather also played a significant role in the outcome of the battle. The British trenches became waterlogged and, as one British observer noted: 'by the continued Rains and Water in the trenches, the most of our Arms were out of order' (Gipson, VI, p. 39). At around 8.00 pm on 3 July, Villiers called for a possible negotiated settlement. Villiers emphasized that he had carried out his attack not because a state of war existed, but to avenge the death of his brother. He also promised that he would allow the British troops to march back to Virginia without harassment from the Indians. Two British officers, Captains Van Braam and Stobo, were to serve as hostages in return for the French prisoners taken on 27 May.

The terms were agreed and on the morning of 4 July, the French marched in to take possession of Fort Necessity. During this transition, the Indians decided to attack the British troops, scalping and killing several men. The French officers and men did little to stop them. While this incident was minor compared to the outrages that were to follow at Fort William Henry in 1757, it clearly demonstrated the problems inherent in promising protection from the Indians following surrender.

The British force marched slowly but in good order towards Wills Creek. The French had effectively forced them out of the Ohio River valley, and Villiers finished the job by destroying Fort Necessity and withdrawing to Fort Duquesne. This defeat galvanized the British government, prompting the decision to deploy British Regular regiments to the Ohio River area. Regular regiments were already stationed in Nova Scotia, and the Fort Duquesne incident convinced British leaders that their presence was required elsewhere. As a result, this engagement was one of the last waged against the French without a sizable British Regular Army presence.

The French and British armies in North America

Warfare in the mid- to late-18th century was characterized by two dissimilar fighting styles, commonly known as linear warfare and irregular or frontier-style warfare. The first was the traditional style in which battles were fought in Europe, whilst the second arose in response to the particular demands of fighting on the North American frontier.

Soldiers of all armies were armed with the flintlock musket, but how they were used differed depending on the style of warfare employed. In any situation, the weapon's range was only 200–300 paces, so no style was developed that was based on the need for accurate fire. Extending the usefulness of the musket during this period was the development of the socket bayonet, which permitted firing with the bayonet already fixed on the musket barrel. The socket bayonet could be attached before troops went into battle, permitting troops to go directly from short-range firing to hand-to-hand combat.

Linear warfare

Given the relative inaccuracy of the flintlock musket, the linear or continental style was designed to maximize its effectiveness. Troops were intended to deploy in a line and deliver a synchronized volley of fire against the opposing line of enemy troops. By training soldiers to fire simultaneously, leaders hoped to offset the musket's inaccuracy with sheer volume of coordinated fire. To accomplish this quickly and effectively required intensive training, not only in firing techniques, but also to enable troops to march overland in column formation, and then rapidly deploy into lines using a series of complicated maneuvers.

The deployment of the front line of troops, or frontage, was determined by the terrain of the battlefield and the position of the enemy. As armies came within sight of one another, each side attempted to maneuver to flank the enemy's position, enabling them to deliver a devastating fire on the enemy, either when they were already in line or attempting to deploy. The battalion deployed in either two, three, or four lines, depending upon the army. The idea was that the forward line fired, then moved back to reload their muskets. They would be replaced by the second line, which would repeat the process and then be followed by the third line and so on.

The French Army deployed its battalions into four lines, with a frontage of 162 men. French battalions were drawn up into 10 companies, consisting of eight fusilier, one grenadier, and one light company. The British Army deployed its battalions into three lines, also with 10 companies of soldiers. The British deployed nine line companies and one grenadier company. As the war progressed they switched to eight line companies, one grenadier company, and one light infantry company. The British frontage was 260 men; some experts argue that this gave the British an advantage by providing a bigger volley, while others claim that the French system was more compact and more maneuverable, and thus superior. In 1758, the British expanded their frontage even further by deploying their battalions in only two lines.

The line of fire was also varied, depending on the situation. The officers would assess the battle situation and order the men either to fire one synchronized volley from the entire line, or a series of volleys from the end of the wings to the center (or vice versa), known as platoon firing. The British Army, for example, divided the men into

This image of the Battle of the Plains of Abraham shows the two different styles of warfare. (National Army Museum, Chelsea)

companies that would fire as one unit. The men in each company were then divided into two platoons, which could fire either as two individual units or one larger one. As described above, battalion firing would begin either in the center or on the wings, hitting the enemy at different locations. It was common for both sides to fire at least one or two coordinated volleys before the battle deteriorated into men firing at will. This was partly due to the fact that the powder and noise of battle often made the soldiers deaf. Fire commands were normally communicated by the battalion drummers, but the escalation of battle made the drums difficult to hear.

The ability to deliver a coordinated heavy volley, and preferably more than one, on the main body of the enemy line was paramount to an army's successful performance. The main intention of this tactic was to create havoc and disorder within the enemy's ranks. A successful volley could break enemy lines, and the firing side would attempt to capitalize on the confusion by advancing on the enemy position. The infantry advance would force the other side to attempt to withdraw, while the advancing side closed in with bayonets to engage in hand to hand fighting. Often units failed to hold the line in the face of a bayonet charge, escalating the disorder and confusion in the ranks of the side under attack.

Troop discipline was critical. Soldiers were drilled exhaustively in the complex procedures involved in deployment, firing, and reloading. In addition to mastering the various techniques, discipline also required troops to stand to attention under enemy fire, retaining a cohesive line while being shot at close range, and returning fire only when ordered to do so. The opposing sides viewed one another as single, massive targets, and soldiers were expected to behave accordingly, functioning as parts of a whole. It was common for a soldier to require 18 months of training to perform the various drills required, and most generals felt it took five years to create a well-trained soldier capable of withstanding the rigors of battle. Contrary to popular perception, the regular soldier of the 18th century was highly trained and proficient; in fact, some rulers' tactics to avoid battle when they were

Rogers' Rangers Officer by Gerry Embleton.

outnumbered or outmaneuvered was due to their unwillingness to risk losing costly and valued regular soldiers.

Artillery was also used in linear warfare of this period, principally as siege weaponry, although smaller pieces were used in infantry battles. These were employed as fire support and also served as markers to indicate divisions between battalions drawing up in linear formation. During the French-Indian War, artillery was used during the small number of linear-style battles, but not to the same extent as in Europe. It was more likely to be used in a conventional manner during sieges of the forts in the North American interior, as these engagements operated in more traditional Continental fashion.

The terrain where most of the North American engagements were fought prohibited the use of cavalry. If there had been engagements in the south, cavalry might have been required, but the heavily forested frontier made operating on horseback both difficult and dangerous. Some senior officers rode to battle on horseback, but tended to dismount before leading a charge.

Irregular warfare

The French-Indian War was instrumental in the further development of a new style of fighting, known as irregular warfare. This approach was characterized by the use of lightly armed troops who could march easily in heavily wooded terrain and fight in small, flexible units. This system was not an entirely North American phenomenon; the Austrians, British, French and Prussians had employed light troops in the European theater of the Seven Years' War. However, the majority of the fighting in North America took place in woodlands, and this necessitated the development and deployment of light troops and other specialists, such as bateaux men (pilots of whale boats and canoes) and Indian scouts, in much greater numbers than had ever been used before.

The Indians of North America were excellent woodsmen; their warriors were skilled not only in fighting one another in forested terrain, but also in hunting in the same woodlands. The frontier populations of both the French and British colonies had also grown adept at maneuvering and fighting in the woods; frontiersmen had extensive contact, both positive and negative, with local Indian populations. In addition, many men were traders or hunters, used to marching overland into harsh territory. Not everyone was an expert however; in fact, a large proportion of people in North America, both recently-arrived Europeans and colonists living in the more developed areas, were utterly unfamiliar with woodland operations.

The North American terrain and conditions dictated not only the strategies of the war but also its progress. Roads and tracks were minimal and poorly developed, and the armies had to take the time (and possess the capability) to build roads as they progressed, as well as forts to protect the roads once completed. Given these conditions, lakes and rivers were ready-made conduits for the movement of men and supplies, and both sides made use of them whenever possible. The ability to move troops and re-supply forward units efficiently was critical to success in the field. The French forces were able to rely on a supply network that operated largely over waterways. The British more often had to build new roads and forts to secure their supply lines, and over time their skills increased through repeated employment. Despite limited opportunity, the British military also performed well in moving both troops and supplies over waterways.

While both France and England had a core of woodland expertise among their fighting men, each side perceived that the war was not going to be won solely on familiarity with the ways of the woods and the Indians. Strategy for both sides involved deploying large numbers of regular troops from Europe who would be able to wage a traditional linear-style battle when terrain permitted. The senior commanders of both armies recognized, to varying degrees, the usefulness of the irregular troops, but preferred linear-style engagements to provide a decisive conclusion to the conflict. In the end, however, the ways in which each side attempted to reform its army to adapt to new conditions in North America proved to be the critical factor in determining a victor.

The following section is an examination of the two military forces involved in the French and Indian War. This will include consideration of the regular forces: their assets, weaknesses, and attempts to reform. The local colonial, militia, and provincial forces will also be discussed. Finally, the fighting capabilities of the Indian

Light Infantryman, 1759 by Gerry Embleton.

participants, as well as their alliances with both sides, will be assessed.

Great Britain

The British Army had four different Commanders-in-Chief over the course of the war in North America. Some, such as Major General Jeffrey Amherst, were successful in battle, while others, such as Lieutenant General John Campbell, Earl Loudon, made a less obvious but more profound organizational impact upon the army. Loudon, while not as successful as Amherst, deserves credit for laying the foundations that gave the Army victory in the campaigns of 1758–60. Although he was only in command during 1756–57, his tenure was marked by significant reforms in methods of supply and tactical development of the regular army.

Loudon centralized the system of supplies for British regular and provincial soldiers to a degree previously unheard of in the Thirteen Colonies. As a result of his restructuring efforts, soldiers were consistently able to receive adequate uniforms and arms – the minimum required for undertaking active service. Main storehouses were created at Halifax, New York, and Albany.

Loudon also recognized that transportation of supplies to troops in the field was necessary for success, and set out to reform the army's systems accordingly. The army had previously relied upon local wagoneers to move supplies forward. This system was unreliable and forced the army to rely upon civilians who were often unwilling to venture very far into the woods. Loudon replaced this system with a corps of army wagons, and undertook a road improvement program. He also appreciated the potential advantages of using waterways for transportation, and delegated John Bradstreet, a leader of armed boatmen, to investigate alternative plans of moving material. This led to an initiative to build a fleet of standardized supply boats piloted by armed and experienced boatmen. A program of creating portages was also undertaken to facilitate the forward movement of supplies. The army and navy also built sloops to move supplies from coastal cities upriver to the Army's major staging areas.

Following the defeats of 1755 and 1756, British Army leaders realized that the troops, in their present state of training and equipment, were not capable of effective operation in the forests of North America. It would be necessary to train and equip men specifically for these conditions; troops would be so equipped as to enable them to maneuver more efficiently in difficult terrain, and would be trained to move in formations other than the large columns used in the linear-style of warfare. Soldiers trained in these unconventional methods were commonly known as rangers.

The concept of rangers did not originate with the onset of the Seven Years' War; ranger troops are recorded as being raised as early as 1744, when a unit named Gorham's Rangers

(after its founder, John Gorham), was raised in Nova Scotia. When war broke out in North America in 1754, the number of rangers in Nova Scotia was increased, at the expense of the British government. In 1755, a second group of rangers was organized, consisting of men from the frontiers of New York and New England. This group, raised and commanded by Major Robert Rogers, took their name, Rogers' Rangers, from him. The ranger corps quickly demonstrated their value in both skirmishes and scouting expeditions on the frontier, but some members of the military establishment remained skeptical, considering the ranger units too expensive to justify their continued existence.

During his tenure as Commander-in-Chief, Loudon, encouraged regular soldiers and officers to attach themselves to the ranger corps to learn methods of forest fighting. He set up a training cadre of 50 rangers at Fort Edward to support this suggestion. Despite attempts such as this to curb the numbers of rangers by creating 'regular' light infantry, the numbers of Rogers' Rangers continued to rise. By 1759 there were six companies of rangers, comprising more than 1,000 men, all financed by the British government.

Loudon decided to create units that would be made up of regulars who would receive special ranger-type training as well as instruction in traditional linear methods. He expected, with this initiative, to manage cost and discipline issues simultaneously: the first by training the same men for different types of warfare, and the second by instilling the 'regular' discipline that was thought to be lacking in rangers. In the event, Loudon's scheme took shape in two different forms. The 60th Regiment of Foot was raised initially from the frontier peoples of Pennsylvania and Virginia, with the intent that the regiment would embody the spirit and abilities of the frontiersman, tempered by the discipline of the regular soldier. Four battalions of the 60th were raised; the 1st and 4th were deployed more often in frontier fighting situations, and fought in successful engagements in Pennsylvania and New York. The 2nd and 3rd battalions served most of

British soldier of the 60th Royal American Regiment
(Osprey Publishing)

their time as regular linear soldiers, and saw action at Louisbourg and Quebec.

Two other regiments were raised under a different interpretation of Loudon's initiative, and these were to have a greater influence on the army as a whole. The 55th and 80th Regiments of Foot were raised specifically as light infantry. They were trained in the tactics used by the ranger corps, but were also subjected to the discipline imposed upon regular troops. (Rangers were not expected to conform to the same standards of discipline as other Army units.) As a result of this successful development, by 1759 all regular British Army regiments, including the 60th, had adopted a light infantry company. These could be deployed as needed in specific situations; their uniforms, weaponry, and tactical training were adapted for marching in the woods, fighting skirmishing actions, and carrying out ambushes in the manner of Indians and rangers.

Two accounts demonstrate the range and effects of these reforms. The first is a manual, published in Philadelphia in 1759, which discusses the specifics involved in waging war in North America, including operating in the forest:

> [I]n passing through close or wooded country … I would have the regiment march two deep, in four columns … having small parties of light infantry advanced [one] hundred paces in their front; but the main party of the light infantry should be on the flanks … [I]f the front should be attacked, the grenadiers and light infantry will be sufficient to keep the enemy in play till the regiment is formed (Military Treatise, pp. 66–67).

In the second account, William Amherst, brother of Jeffrey, notes in his journal a typical training day for two regiments in 1758, including a description of a new firing sequence to be used by British columns if they were attacked on the march in the woods:

> the advanced party if attacked, the two platoons marching abreast, the left platoon fires singly, every man, the right platoon keeps recovered, both platoons moving on very slowly and inclining to the right (William Amherst, pp. 40–41).

The aim of such exercises was to accustom the soldiers to wooded conditions, and so neutralize the fear of Indian tactics.

The innovations made in training and equipment improved British performance in the forest but it did not make them invincible. On several occasions during both the French-Indian War and the subsequent Indian uprising of 1763–64, British troops were ambushed and suffered accordingly. The British regular soldier became the equal in the forest of his French equivalent, although the Indian remained, for the most part, the master of forest operation. This expertise, however, was offset by a lack of discipline and coordinated command and control expertise, which benefited the regulars on both sides. Most important, the average British soldier had, by 1759, largely lost his fear of operating in the forest, having received the training required to cope with most situations.

The average British battalion numbered from 500–900 men. Numbers fluctuated due to battle casualties, illness, and desertion. In 1754 there were no British line regiments stationed in the Thirteen Colonies, only in Nova Scotia and the Caribbean. The Thirteen Colonies had seven regular units named Independent Companies, which were posted along areas of the South Carolina and New York frontiers. By 1757, more than 14,000 regulars had been deployed to the Thirteen Colonies as a result of the conflict in North America. By 1759, the peak of regular establishment in North America, nearly 24,000 men were under arms. The British Army included mostly regular line regiments with 10 companies (eight line, one grenadier and one light infantry). There were also dedicated ad hoc light infantry and grenadier battalions.

British military officials had an additional reserve force to draw upon for the French-Indian War: the colonial provincials. These were units whom the Colonies were requested to raise, to serve alongside the regular forces. Some military officials considered them more of a burden than an asset, principally because, unlike regular soldiers, provincial soldiers were only called for one campaign season at a time, and then returned to their homes. This created the impression that because provincial soldiers were not professionals, they were not subjected to the same harsh discipline and rules that the regulars endured, and that they were not, therefore, true soldiers. The provincials, on their side, considered regular soldiers ignorant of how to operate in the forest and the conditions of the frontier. Such beliefs created a rivalry that persisted throughout the war period, each side regarding the other as unfit to fight in various combat situations.

During the first years of the war, relations between provincials and regulars were further strained. The first article of the Rules and Articles of War of the British Army of this period stated that 'a provincial soldier serving with regulars ceased to be governed by colonial disciplinary measures but became subject to the mutiny act' (Pargellis, p.84). This stipulation was created by British military

authorities who envisioned no more than a few provincial companies serving with the regulars. It meant, in theory, that provincial soldiers serving alongside regulars were subject to the same strict regulations and discipline. In practice, however, there were likely to be discrepancies in treatment. Loudon reported one instance where 'a private of the 60th found guilty of mutiny received 1,000 lashes whereas a private of a Massachusetts [provincial] regiment got 500 for the same offence' (Loudon, 3 September 1757). Braddock's defeat in 1755 changed the situation considerably by demonstrating the immediate need for a large number of soldiers. As a result, the number of provincial soldiers required also increased dramatically.

The increased need for provincial troops brought about one beneficial change in their situation. Previously, commissioned officers in the provincial forces, even as high as the rank of General, were degraded to the level of senior captain when serving alongside regular forces in the field. This was a major source of resentment for the provincial forces. Loudon was uninterested in resolving this issue with the colonial governments, and no changes were made until after he was removed from command. William Pitt, Secretary of State (with control of the war and foreign affairs and later the leader of the British government), amended the ruling so that provincial officers retained their rank, but were junior to regular officers of equivalent and higher rank. Pitt considered this necessary to appease the colonial governments and convince them to recruit more men for the campaigns. Even though the British government ultimately funded colonial units, they had to rely on the colonial governments' efforts to fill the ranks. In the event, his tactic was successful; the colonial governments provided more soldiers in 1758 and 1759, after the ruling was changed, than they had previously.

Despite this initiative and the rising number of provincial troops, regular soldiers continued to distrust their fighting abilities, and only grudgingly would they concede that provincials made a contribution. It was true that provincials were unlikely to have the stamina to sustain the rigors of a linear-style battle, since they did not have the same level of training or discipline as regular troops. There was the occasional compliment; as noted by a regular officer in 1759 :

the provincial regiments, under arms today, to be perfected in the manoeuvres contained in the regulations of the 20th of June ... [T]hey [provincials] made a good performance, performed well, and gave great satisfaction (Knox, p. 486).

Major General Amherst gave a reluctant-sounding compliment when speaking of the provincials in 1759 at Fort Edward:

[they] began to grow sickly and lose some men; they are growing homesick but much less so than ever they have been on any other campaigns (Amherst, 22 September 1759).

France

On the other side of the conflict, the French were spending comparable time arguing over strategy and the abilities of their regulars to wage war along the frontier. Major General Louis-Joseph Montcalm, who commanded the French regular forces from 1756 until his death in 1759, disagreed firmly with the governor-general of New France, Pierre Francois de Rigaud Vaudreuil on issues of strategy. There was often considerable antagonism between colonial-born (such as Vaudreuil) and French-born officials (such as Montcalm); the colonials perceived visitors as high-handed interlopers who did not understand the issues particular to the colonial setting. The French government had clearly established the lines of command – Vaudreuil was unquestionably senior to Montcalm – but in practice this had no effect on mitigating tensions or resolving proposals of conflicting strategies. Unlike Loudon in the British Colonies, neither man was removed from service when tensions flared, and the situation escalated. Each man

accused the other of interfering in issues of strategy. Marquis de Vaudreuil favored a guerilla campaign along the frontier, and dismissed the ability of the French regulars to adapt to the necessities of waging war in the forest. Montcalm recognized the value of militia and Indians in forest operations, but still believed that the war would ultimately be decided by regular troops.

Montcalm did understand the issues of supply and scouting involved in fighting in the woods. A master strategist, he recognized early that the British were going to outnumber his forces, and decided upon a defensive strategy that would allow him to launch pre-emptive strikes whenever opportunity permitted. Having decided on this plan of action, he implemented it early in the campaign with surprise attacks on the British forts at Oswego and Fort William Henry in 1756 and 1757. He succeeded in overwhelming the troops guarding all the forts, and forced them to surrender. He did not stay put, but destroyed the forts and moved. It was

Marquis de Vaudreuil. (Public Archives of Canada)

Louis-Joseph Montcalm. (Ann Ronan Picture Library)

a bold strategy, and effectively knocked the British off balance for a time early on. In 1758, however, the situation changed dramatically. The British had begun to learn the art of war in the forest and had created a supply network that could carry their armies over difficult terrain. On the other side, the French forces received no reinforcements after 1757, thanks to the Royal Navy blockade. Montcalm was forced to guard a vast frontier with less than one-third of the regular troops that the British had at their disposal. He continued to take gambles; some of them paid dividends, such as the decision to deploy most of his regulars to Fort Carillon in 1758 as described below. But from 1758, Montcalm

Fusilier, Compagnies Franches de la Marine by Michael Roffe. (Osprey Publishing)

Grenadier, Regiment de Languedoc by Michael Roffe. (Osprey Publishing)

was constantly on the defensive, attempting to stem the rising tide of British attacks.

The French and British forces were organized along similar lines – a mixture of regulars, militia, and Indian allies. The first group of regulars that served in New France was the *troupes de la marine* or marines. When war broke out between France and Britain in 1754, no French regular line infantry units were initially deployed to North America. The marines had been serving under the command of the French Navy in New France for many years before the outbreak of hostilities. The men and officers were recruited in France for colonial service, and encouraged to remain in North America after their terms of enlistment ended. The marines served along the frontiers of New France, as well as in the trading centers, and were organized along lines similar to those of the British Independent Companies; their detachments were organized into company sized units. Numbers within companies fluctuated from 50–75 men, and as of 1750, there were 30 companies deployed in New France. By 1757, 64 companies had been deployed in Quebec and Cape Breton, with another 30 companies stationed in the Louisiana territory. Companies from Louisiana were involved in fighting in the Ohio River area during the course of the war. Marines, while commonly considered regular soldiers in the colonial administration, also had considerable experience of operating in the woods based upon years of deployment on the frontier.

By 1757, only 12 battalions of French regulars, known as the *troupes de terre* and numbering just over 6,000 men, had been shipped to North America. Eight of the battalions saw service with Montcalm in the Canada and Western theaters, and four were sent to Louisbourg to bolster its defenses. French regular soldiers were generally willing to learn some of the bush fighting tactics used by the Canadian militia and Indians and, like their British counterparts, often attached themselves to small raiding parties to learn the tactics of the woods.

During the first years of the war, the French regulars performed very well in battle. Discipline was very good; Montcalm cited only two courts martial during the period from 1756–58. Montcalm also commended the condition and performance of his troops, describing the Royal-Roussillon regiment as 'well supplied and well disciplined' (Sautai, p. 23). However, as French strategy changed in the wake of the effective British naval blockade and troops were increasingly left to fend for themselves in New France, discipline and desertion became greater problems. The performance of the French regulars at the Battle of the Plains of Abraham indicated that fire discipline had deteriorated noticeably from previous standards. To their credit, the French regulars continued to perform very well, particularly considering that they were vastly outnumbered by the British, suffered from unreliable provision of supplies, and became increasingly aware that grand strategy in the larger conflict had shifted attention and resources away from them. In light of these obstacles, American historian Francis Parkman commended the French Army in North America 'for enduring gallantry, officers and men alike deserve nothing but praise' (Parkman, p. 215).

The Canadian militia was a major asset to the French commanders. Unlike provincial troops in the Thirteen Colonies, the Canadian militia was geared for war. Montcalm, apparently recognizing their value, described Canadians as

born soldiers, from the age of 16 … on the rolls of militia. Boatmen and good shots, hunters … [T]hey excelled in forest war and ambushes (Sautai, p. 16).

This idea of a citizenry geared for war was not unique to New France and occurred often in Europe; notably similar to the Canadians were the Croat populations along the Austrian/Turkish borderlands. While militiamen were not sufficiently trained to rebuff a full-scale linear-style attack, they were more than proficient in wilderness fighting and scouting. Militiamen in New France were generally assigned to protect forts and remote outposts, a practice that was also common in the Thirteen Colonies. They were also assigned flank and scouting activities, either performed alone or as part of a larger regular column.

The number of militiamen raised in New France throughout the war period never exceeded 15,000 men per year. Similar to British provincials, they returned home after each campaigning season; many men returned to the militia year after year, as the threat to New France increased. The Thirteen Colonies provided a larger number of provincial soldiers, but they were not of the same quality as Canadian militiamen. Montcalm claimed that relations between his regulars and the militia and Indians were very cordial; in 1757 he declared that 'our troops … live in perfect union with the Canadians and savages' (Sautai, p. 26). Some of his junior officers disagreed with this assessment; one officer noted in 1758 that:

> *when the French had won the battle, confidence returned … [T]hey regained their Canadian spirits and busied themselves only in ways of taking away from the French [Regular] troops the glory of an action which it appeared difficult to attribute to anyone else* (Bougainville, p. 239).

There was tension between French and Canadian officers, principally on questions of tactics. Some French officers preferred to use linear-style tactics, and believed that the Canadian soldiers and officers were no better than the Indians. The Canadian officers, for their part, felt on more than one occasion that French troops were not suited for frontier warfare. This caused friction, as it did within the British forces.

Indians

Both Great Britain and France sought the allegiance of the numerous Indian tribes living along the frontiers of the European colonies in North America. Indian warriors were expert forest fighters, unsurpassed in their skill at both ambushing and scouting. Their reputation as warriors struck fear into the hearts of civilians and soldiers alike. A British grenadier reported outside Quebec in 1759 that 'all the grenadiers crossed over to the island of Orleans … [T]he Indians attacked us very smartly' (*Journal of the Expedition to the River St. Lawrence*, 21 July 1759). This was only intensified by their willingness to shift their alliances from one side to the other as the fortunes of each waxed and waned. Many Indian warriors would disappear from a campaign if they felt their side was losing or there was a chance of plunder in another part of the frontier. They were considered untrustworthy by European troops, and criticized for their opportunistic decisions to side with the strongest power.

Of course, both Britain and France also tried to use such opportunism to their own advantage, trying more than once to undermine existing treaties between the enemy side and its Indian allies. In battle, Indians excelled in gaining intelligence for their European commanders, as well as setting ambushes. However, when faced with continental-style fighting in the open they tended to break very easily. They also lacked the stamina and planning skills to carry out a siege of a small post. The Indian Uprising of 1763–64 is an example.

The French tended to be more successful in winning the allegiance of Indians. This is partly due to the fact that the French

Colonel William Johnson, Superintendent of Indian affairs for the British Crown. (Albany Institute of History and Art)

Huron by Michael Roffe. (Osprey Publishing)

Indian lands along the frontier. Tension was thus correspondingly greater. The French formed alliances with five major Indian tribes: the Hurons, Ottawas, Wyandots, Miamis, and Algonquins. The principal British-Indian alliance was with the members of the Five (later Six) Nations of the Iroquois. The original five nations were the Oneidas, Mohawks, Senecas, Onondagas, and Cayugas, and were subsequently joined by the Tuscaroras. The French repeatedly attempted to win over one of the Iroquois nations to their cause throughout the course of the war, but were consistently thwarted by the efforts of Lieutenant Colonel William Johnson, chief Indian agent for the British Crown. The Senecas did later become dissatisfied with the British alliance, but this was later and for other reasons; the dispute will be covered in the Indian Uprising section.

On the whole both sides tended to accept their Indian allies as a necessity, and tried to regulate their behavior by imposing harsh penalties for failure to follow orders. One characteristic situation happened in 1757, when the French-allied Indians killed a number of the British civilians who had surrendered at Fort William Henry. French regulars had to restrain their allies with the threat of violence if they did not stop the killing. Some senior British commanders loathed using Indian allies against European soldiers or civilians. In the end, warfare increasingly utilized more conventional methods, and both sides relied less upon the services of Indians. Equally significant, following the French defeat at Quebec in 1759, many Indians decided to leave French service, fearing British reprisals upon their villages.

presence in North America was smaller than the British presence. Many Indians only came in contact with Canadian traders, who they did not consider to be encroaching upon their territory. British colonists, however, were a larger population, seeking land as well as trading opportunities in the

Entry of the regular soldiers

Although formal declarations of war were not exchanged between France and Great Britain until 1756, the deployment of two British Regular regiments toward Fort Duquesne and the operations against Fort Beausejour in Nova Scotia, Fort Niagara, and Crown Point marked the formal outbreak of the war in North America. The narrative describing the progress of the conflict will be divided into years and subdivided into regions. The fighting that took place in the Ohio River region and Pennsylvania will be referred to as the Western theater. The fighting in the Lake George, Lake Champlain, and western New York regions will be referred to as the New York theater. The Canadian theater will cover operations in Nova Scotia, Cape Breton, and Quebec.

In October 1754, the British government, headed by Thomas Pelham-Holles, Duke of Newcastle, ordered the reinforcement of the Thirteen Colonies with regular troops in response to increasing tension in the Ohio River valley. The orders called for the transportation of the 44th and 48th Regiments of Foot to Virginia, under the command of Major General Edward Braddock, who was to be in overall command of all troops in North America. The two regiments were below strength and officials decided to fill the companies with locally recruited men upon reaching the American colonies. Two additional regiments, the 50th and 51st Foot, were to be raised in their entirety in North America.

The dispatch of British regulars only alerted the French to follow suit. Beyond the companies of marines (regulars) already deployed in New France, the French dispatched 3,000 regulars from the line regiments of La Reine, Artois, Guienne, Languedoc, and Bearn. They were all under the supreme command of Baron de Dieskau. These regulars were unable to reach Fort Duquesne in time to support its defense, but were deployed to protect other vulnerable positions afterwards.

The British strategy for 1755 was that General Braddock and his two regiments, along with provincial units, would march on and seize Fort Duquesne from the French. Meanwhile, the second-in-command in North America, Governor Shirley of Massachusetts, was to march with the 50th and 51st regiments, as well as various provincial units, to seize the French fort at Niagara. Colonel Johnson was to march from Albany against the French Fort St. Frederic at Crown Point. Finally, Lieutenant Colonel Robert Monckton, a British Regular, was to lead a force of 2,000 militia and 200 regulars against Fort Beausejour in Nova Scotia.

War of the forest and fortress

Western theater

Braddock, along with the 44th and 48th Foot, arrived in Virginia in March 1755. By May, the force, regulars, provincials, and Royal Artillery, was assembling at Fort Cumberland, Wills Creek. They were delayed from leaving on schedule by the lack of supplies forthcoming from the various colonial governments and the need for additional recruits for both regular and provincial units. The British expedition, finally fully assembled and provisioned, marched out from Fort Cumberland on 10 June.

The British government was confident that the infusion of regular troops would ensure victory, but failed to recognize that a different type of war was in store. Braddock's only experience of warfare was on the European Continent, and he was not fully aware of the potential pitfalls involved in waging war over difficult, hilly, and forested terrain. His French adversaries had a better understanding of how to effectively mix the discipline and training of French regulars (marines) with the more unorthodox methods of the Canadian militia and allied Indians.

The British expedition averaged only 6 km (four miles) a day on the march, slowed down by the wagons and the condition of the road. On 18 June, the force reached Little Meadows, where Braddock decided to split his force. He would lead 1,200 picked men ahead of the baggage and rest of the men, the vast majority of whom were provincial troops. A specialist unit of rangers was put under the command of Lieutenant Colonel Thomas Gage to advance forward of the column and protect it from surprise attack. Braddock and Gage set off, and were soon set upon by French scouts and Indians. The rangers and other flank troops successfully subdued repeated French and Indian ambush attempts. Braddock, Gage,

and 1,200 men reached the remains of Fort Necessity on 25 June.

The French garrison at Fort Duquesne numbered more than 100 regulars, 200 Canadian militia, and nearly 1,000 allied Indians. The British column crossed the Monongahela River about 32 km (20 miles)

east of the fort in early July, but shortly had to cross back, frustrated by the terrain. In the meantime, Captain de Beaujeu assembled an attack force of most of the French regulars, plus 100 Canadians and a sizeable Indian force, and led them out of Fort Duquesne. On 6 July forward elements of both armies met and skirmished. On 8 July, Braddock's column crossed the river for the second time just below Fort Duquesne. The crossing went without difficulty, one British observer describing how the 'main body cross with colours flying, drums beating and fifes playing' (*JSAHQR*, 61, p. 202).

The French force came within sight of the advance guards of the British column, and fighting broke out at midday. The British formed a skirmish line and opened fire on the French, killing Captain de Beaujeu in the opening volley. A Captain Dumas assumed command and decided to deploy the troops along the sides of the British column in the woods, trapping the advance guard of Gage's force in a cross-fire from the French and Indian troops. Gage, instead of pushing forward, decided to

Braddock's march to Fort Duquesne. (Ann Ronan Picture Library)

Braddocks column under attack. The image is viewed from the positions of the French and allied Indians firing into the British positions. (State Historical Society of Wisconsin)

fall back. The French and Indians had seized the crucial high ground, and as the British troops withdrew, the French and Indians continued to pour fire into their ranks. A Royal Artillery officer described the scene:

the first fire the enemy gave was in front and they likewise attacked the piquets in flank, so that in a few minutes the grenadiers were nearly cut to pieces and drove into great confusion ... [When t]he main body heard that the front was attacked they instantly advanced ... [T]he enemy attacked the main body ... [The British] engaged them but could not see whom they fired at [as] the trees were thick ... [S]oldiers [were] encouraged to take the hill but they had been intimidated and many officers declared they never saw above 5 of the enemy at one time ... [Braddock] divided the men into small parties but the main part of the officers were either killed or wounded and in short the soldiers were totally deaf to the command of the few officers

that were left unhurt (JSAHQR, 61, pp. 202–203).

After three hours of fighting, the British column began to fall back to the river. More than 800 of their men and officers were killed or wounded, including General Braddock, who had been mortally wounded. The French lost three officers killed and four wounded, plus 10 regulars and Canadians killed. It is estimated that the Indians lost between 20 and 100 warriors. The remains of the British

column reached Fort Necessity on 17 July, and from there the army made a further withdrawal to Fort Cumberland. The immediate threat to Fort Duquesne had been nullified, at least for 1755.

It is true that Braddock lacked knowledge of warfare in North America, but as he undertook very good flank protection on the march, his inexperience was only part of the reason for the crushing British defeat. The battle was, effectively, a collision between the two armies. The French and Indians had the advantage of the high ground, which Gage should have seized. Braddock attempted to seize the high ground by force, but the French and Indians were too well established and the troops were beaten back mercilessly. Any British general of the period would have had a difficult time attempting to rectify the situation, and there is nothing to indicate that a provincial commander would have fared any better. Captain Dumas, the French commander, deserves full credit for sound and innovative action at the right moment.

New York theater

Following General Braddock's death, Governor (Major General) Shirley became commander-in-chief of the British forces in North America. Shirley was designated to lead the expedition against Fort Niagara, primarily using the two newly raised regular regiments filled with raw recruits and various provincial units. He assembled his force in late July. The plan called for the column to travel overland and by river to Oswego, a British–Indian trading center situated on Lake Ontario. It was more than 321 km (200 miles) from Albany to Oswego, and a further 241 km (150 miles) to Fort Niagara via Lake Ontario.

Shirley and the major part of his expedition arrived at Oswego on 17 August. They encountered no opposition, either en route or when they arrived. The difficult passage to Oswego, followed by numerous delays in the arrival of supplies and troops once there, prevented Shirley moving on toward Fort Niagara as quickly as planned. The last troops arrived in Oswego on 2 September, but supply problems continued and desertions had begun. In the interim, the French, taking advantage of the delay, had moved troops to Fort Frontenac, on the north side of Lake Ontario, and to other posts to protect Niagara. Shirley, aware of the growing threat from the north and the decreasing time left to lay siege to the fort, decided to call off the attack until the next campaign season and build up defenses in the Oswego area instead.

At around the same time, Lieutenant Colonel Johnson headed from Albany towards Lake George with 2,000 provincial soldiers, under orders to construct Fort Edward on the Hudson River, south of Lake George. Upon completion of this task, he was to proceed to Lake George, sail north, and attack the French positions on the north side of the lake. From there, he was supposed to continue to Fort St. Frederic (Crown Point) at the southern end of Lake Champlain, just north of Lake George. Johnson reached the southern end of Lake George in late August, where he received reports from Indian scouts that the French were in position at Ticonderoga (later Fort Carillon, also at the southern end of Lake Champlain) but they had not yet constructed fortifications. Baron Dieskau had heard reports that Johnson was stationed at Fort Edward. He led 3,500 French regulars, militia, and Indians to Ticonderoga, and leaving the majority of these troops there to construct Fort Carillon, took 1,000 regulars, militia, and Indians to attack the British at Fort Edward. As the French forces moved down the lake in bateaux, they realized that Johnson was in fact encamped at the southern end of Lake George, several miles north of where they expected to find him.

The British camp was fortified against possible attack, and the two armies met on 8 September. The French regulars marched in open order towards the camp, but their fire only pounded the felled trees surrounding

the British position. The provincials retaliated with musket and artillery. The French attempted to shift their fire, but were unable to inflict heavy casualties. After a few hours the Canadian and Indian troops melted away, but, as Johnson noted, the '[French regulars] kept their ground and order for some time with great resolution and good conduct' (Gipson, VI, p. 172). Eventually, however, the French began to lose ground, and the provincials seized the advantage, launched a counter-attack, and captured the wounded Dieskau. The battle ended when a relieving force arrived from Fort Edward, forcing a conclusive French withdrawal.

The British and French had each lost more than 200 men in the battle at Lake George. The British campaign towards Fort St. Frederick came to a halt when news was received that the French had begun to fortify Ticonderoga and renamed it Fort Carillon. The British were content with their victory and fortified the southern end of Lake George with the construction of Fort William Henry.

Canadian theater

Ironically, the smallest British expedition was also the most successful of the 1755 campaign season. Lieutenant Colonel Monckton led 2,000 provincials and 280 regulars against the French Fort Beausejour in Nova Scotia. The invasion force sailed from Boston on 26 May for (Fort) Annapolis Royal in Nova Scotia. Artillery and supplies were sent in from Halifax to Fort Lawrence, on the route to the expedition's final destination, in time for the arrival of the Boston contingent on 2 June. The troops stopped just long enough to re-supply, marching out on 4 June toward the fort.

British troops spent the next week clearing the areas surrounding Fort Beausejour of Acadians who were providing support to the French cause. The displaced Acadians flooded toward the fort for protection. Beausejour was manned by a few companies of regulars, plus nearly 1,000 Acadian militia. By 14 June, most of the area around the fort had been cleared and the British artillery was in position to begin the bombardment of the fort. A French observer described how

on the morning of the 16 [June] an enemy bomb exploded on one of the casements to the left of the entrance … [I]t was enough to bring about the surrender of the fort because fire combined with inexperience made everyone in that place give up (Journals of Beausejour, p. 97).

The nearby French Fort Gapereau also capitulated, creating a significant breach in the French strategy of a continuous line of forts from Louisbourg to New Orleans. Aside from the water route toward Quebec, Louisbourg had been utterly cut off by the British action. One lasting, and infamous, legacy of the fighting in Nova Scotia in 1755 was the expulsion of the Acadian population by British authorities. This will be discussed later in the book.

The overall British strategy for 1755 had not been fully executed. The British had been completely stymied in the Ohio River area and had made limited gains in two other campaigns. Only in Nova Scotia had the strategy borne fruit. The fighting in the New York and Western theaters had additionally accelerated the deterioration of relations between regular and provincial troops. Numerous provincial observers were critical of the performance of the regulars with Braddock's expedition, especially after some regulars accidentally mistook Virginian provincials for French troops and fired upon them. Lieutenant Colonel Washington, who was present at the battle on 9 July, commented that 'our poor Virginians behaved like men and died like soldiers' (18 July 1755, *The Writings of George Washington*). The victory at Lake George, also won by provincials, gave further credibility to the colonial belief that British regulars might not be suited to fighting conditions in North America.

1756

The major fighting of 1756 occurred around the British post at Oswego on Lake Ontario. The British were very much on the defensive during 1756, mainly because of their focus on the build-up of provincial and regular units to fight and on smoothing relations between the two groups. The French, even though they were outnumbered in both regular and militia establishments for the remainder of the war, nevertheless launched numerous offensive operations in both 1756 and 1757.

The French command in Canada was largely divided between Marquis de Vaudreuil, who in theory had influence in the deployment of the colonial regulars and militia, and the new commander-in-chief of the French regular forces, Marquis de Montcalm-Gozon de Saint-Veran. The French port of Louisbourg, however, was under the command of neither Montcalm nor Vaudreuil, but that of Chevalier de Augustin Drucour.

Montcalm sailed from France for Quebec on 3 April 1756, accompanied by a reinforcement of two battalions of the Royal-Roussillon and La Sarre regiments. His two senior commanders were Brigadier le Chevalier de Levis and Colonel le Chevalier de Bourlamaque. As Montcalm sailed toward Quebec, war between Great Britain and France was formally declared on 17 May. For the French forces in North America, this did not mean that France would focus her military might on North America. On the contrary, strategy in France was divided between colonial and Continental ambitions, and there was strong sentiment at the French court for devoting the largest military effort to the conflict in Continental Europe. By 1758, the French court had shifted almost completely to a strategy of invading and seizing Hannover, in the hope that it could be used as a bargaining chip for the return of New France, should the British succeed in defeating Montcalm. In any case, even had strategic plans been otherwise, the Royal Navy undertook a very successful blockade,

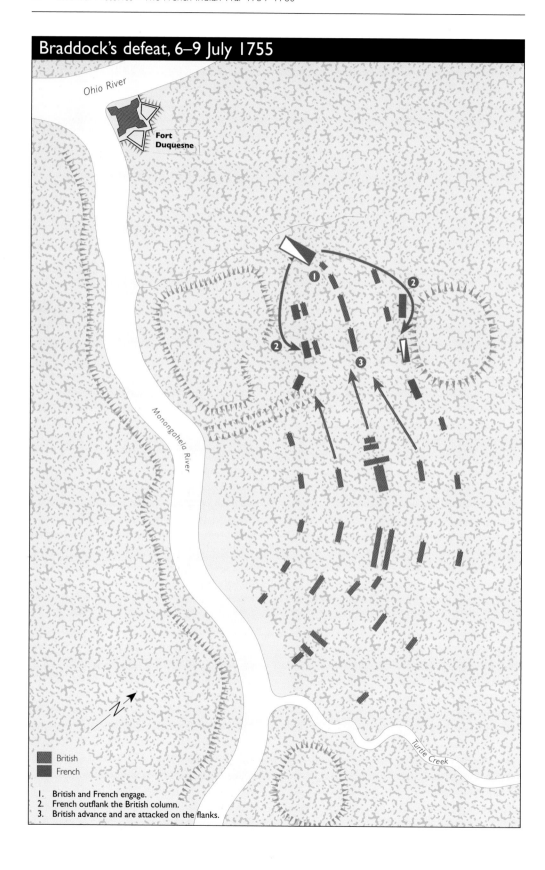

Braddock's defeat, 6–9 July 1755

Ohio River

Fort
Duquesne

Monongahela River

Turtle Creek

British
French

1. British and French engage.
2. French outflank the British column.
3. British advance and are attacked on the flanks.

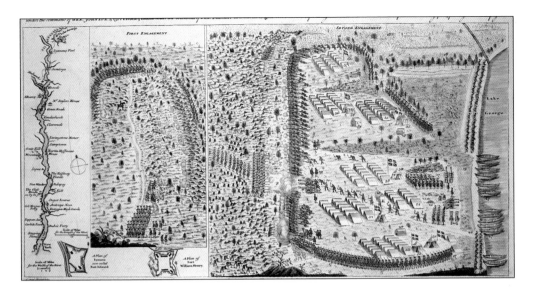

Battle of Lake George 1755. The image illustrates the British fortified camp on the right. Lake George is to the British rear. The French are attacking from the left side of the image. (Anne SK Brown Collection)

bottling up the French fleet in Toulon and Brest and denying the French the opportunity to supply North America with reinforcements. For more information regarding this strategy see Essential Histories, *The Seven Years' War*.

The British government took the opposite strategic approach following the formal outbreak of war, deciding that seizing New France would be an important strategic advantage in the larger world war that began to develop in the spring of 1756. To this end, two more regiments were sent from Great Britain in 1756, accompanied by senior generals, such as Major General James Abercromby, Major General Daniel Webb, and a new commander-in-chief, John Campbell, Earl of Loudon, with orders to rectify the situation that had developed in 1755. British regulars were still not equipped to fight effectively in the forest, and Army leaders had decided to create a new regiment of regulars. The 62nd (later 60th) Regiment of Foot was to be raised in North America from the frontier populations, and its training was designed to combine the discipline of the regulars with the frontier fighting skills of a colonial

militiaman. Although not all of the recruits for this four-battalion regiment originated from the frontier population, this development marked a significant change in policy and an attempt by British regulars to get to grips with the sort of warfare particular to North America.

New York theater

Loudon, his staff, and the regular reinforcements arrived in Albany in late June, where he assumed overall command of the army in North America. As discussed earlier, he was faced immediately with the problems resulting from a Royal Order which decreed all provincial officers (including senior officers such as generals and colonels) were to revert to the senior rank of senior captain when serving alongside regular troops. Loudon met with senior provincial officers and was able to get them to agree to the new edict, but it did nothing to improve relations between the two groups.

A senior British officer, Lieutenant Colonel Burton, was sent to report on the state of the provincial forces stationed at Fort William Henry and Fort Edward. He described the camp at Fort William Henry as 'nastier than anything I could conceive ... a great waste of provisions, the men having just what they please, no great command kept up' (Parkman, p. 233). The regular

View of Fort Beausejour. (Public Archives of Canada)

officer was not being prejudiced. A
Massachusetts doctor, Dr. Thomas Williams,
stationed at Fort William Henry reported:
'we bury five or six a day. Not more than
two thirds of our army fit for duty'
(Parkman, p. 234). The plan for an attack on
Fort Carillon, just beyond the north side of
Lake George, would have to be delayed.

The French feared that the main British
attack would come against them at Fort
Carillon. Montcalm arrived at Fort Carillon
in July, and decided to draw off British
attention from the fort and apply pressure
against Oswego instead. At first this plan
only envisioned a feint attack but in the end
it was to be the major campaign of the
season. A column of 1,000 French regulars,
Canadians, and Indians, under the command
of Coulon de Villiers, was assembled to cut
communications between Oswego and
Albany. They arrived in the area in early July,
where they encountered a column of
provincial troops. The unit numbered just
over 500 men, and was under the command
of Captain John Bradstreet, a New Englander
with a commission in the 62nd (60th) Foot.
Bradstreet's men had arrived in Oswego
with supplies and were returning by boat
to Albany.

On the 3 July, Bradstreet was ambushed
by the French troops. The skirmish lasted for

most of the day, with both sides claiming
victory in the end. The encounter was most
likely a draw, from which both sides were
able to extricate themselves with prisoners
taken but few casualties. The French ambush
did alert the British commanders to the
precarious position that Oswego was in, but
the confusion surrounding Loudon's arrival
and accompanying changes in bureaucracy
meant that a major reinforcement for the
area was not prepared till 12 August. The
44th Regiment of Foot and provincials were
assigned the task of reinforcing Oswego,
where they were sorely needed. They were
not, however, to arrive in time.

Montcalm was already on the move
against Oswego. He had marched out from
Fort Carillon in early July, leaving behind
3,000 men to defend the north end of Lake
George. Montcalm reached Fort Frontenac, at
the northern end of Lake Ontario, on
29 July, and from there he sent ahead a small
detachment of regulars, militia, and Indians
to rendezvous with Villiers near Oswego.
Montcalm, meanwhile, came behind with
the bulk of the force, which landed a mile
from Oswego on 10 August. The French
columns converged on Fort Ontario the
next day.

The garrison at the three forts at Oswego –
Ontario, Pepperell (Oswego), and George –
were commanded by Colonel Mercer. Shirley
had left two locally raised regular regiments

in the area for the winter of 1755–56, and these were divided between forts Ontario and Pepperell. New Jersey provincials were stationed at Fort George, with the total garrison numbering just over 1,500 men. A river separated Fort Ontario from the other two encampments, and it stood on a height overlooking Oswego and Fort George.

The French column was carrying a large contingent of siege artillery for its assault on the three forts. After two days and nights of heavy bombardment, Fort Ontario was shattered. Colonel Mercer ordered the evacuation of Fort Ontario to the western side of the river on 13 August, and the survivors were able to get across to Oswego. Montcalm moved his artillery to the captured heights where Ontario had stood, and on the morning of 14 August, his cannon opened up on the two remaining forts. A column of French and Indian troops crossed the river unopposed under cover of cannon fire. The effect of the artillery fire was described as leaving the British: 'so much exposed that the Enemy could see the buckles in our shoes' (*Journal of the Siege of Oswego*, Military History of Great Britain, for 1756, 1757, p. 38).

After the heavy bombardment in which Colonel Mercer was killed, the remaining officers held a council of war and decided to surrender. In the end the British lost 50 men and the French forces about half that. As with other French victories, the French-allied Indians wrought havoc among the surrendered British soldiers and civilians. Montcalm had to intervene to stop the killing and pillaging after the surrender. The prisoners were transported to Montreal. Montcalm destroyed everything in the area of any value, and then withdrew. His troops redeployed to forts Niagara, Frontenac and Carillon, having decisively entered the conflict in 1756. The offensive defense had paid dividends, keeping the British off balance for another year.

The rest of 1756 passed with small bands of provincials, principally Rogers' Rangers and French Canadian and Indian troops, harassing posts along the frontier. This period

became known as the partisan war. The loss of the 50th and 51st Regiments of Foot at Oswego prompted the renumbering of all British regiments listed above 51, and so the 62nd Regiment of Foot became the 60th.

1757

Similar to 1756, 1757 would be marked by only one major engagement between France and Britain, and again this was fought in the New York theater of operations. The partisan war continued along the frontier, spreading fear among both French and British settlers.

Over the course of 1757, the British reinforced their war effort with more than 11,000 regular troops shipped out from Great Britain. By the end of 1757, 21 battalions of British regulars and seven Independent companies were operating in North America. The British were also able to call upon the colonies for further provincial forces, which were used in increasing numbers to protect lines of communications with forts along the frontier. On the French side, Montcalm received his last major reinforcement in 1757, with the arrival of two battalions of the Regiment de Berry. Montcalm had only eight battalions of regulars (there were 12 in total, but four were stationed at Louisbourg) and 64 companies of colonial regulars, stationed from Louisbourg to New Orleans. He also, like his British counterparts, had a large contingent of militia and a larger number of Indian allies to draw upon for the campaign.

A change of government in Britain in 1757 caused the Newcastle ministry to be replaced, first by William Pitt and William Cavendish, and then, after a short time by a coalition government, the Newcastle-Pitt ministry, in the winter of 1757. The Newcastle-Pitt ministry changed strategy, shifting the British focus to attacking Louisbourg and Quebec, the heart of New France. In response to the new strategic plan, Lord Loudon withdrew a large number of regulars from New York in April and sailed for Halifax. He was further reinforced with

Montcalm surrounded by his men.
(Ann Ronan Picture Library)

newly arrived regular troops from Great
Britain, and was ordered to attack the French
fortress at Louisbourg, in an attempt to open
up Quebec to attack.

Poor intelligence gathering and the
French Navy's continued dominance of its

British naval opposition in the area near
Louisbourg meant that Loudon was unsure
of the size of the French forces. He hesitated
to launch an attack, and by July, the plans
had to be put aside when the Royal Navy
was unable to gain the upper hand in the
region. Montcalm was aware of these
developments, and his scouts reported that
the frontier had been stripped of many

British regulars. Montcalm decided to take advantage of the situation, and prepared to strike at Fort William Henry, at the southern end of Lake George.

New York theater

By July, Montcalm had amassed a large force in and around Fort Carillon and was planning an attack on Fort William Henry before the end of the month. The French attack column was to number 7,500 men, including six regular battalions, marines, militia, and Indians. Montcalm split his force in two; one group of 2,600 men traveled overland, while the other, some 5,000 men traveled in bateaux over the lake. The two forces met at the southern end of the lake on 2 August.

The British force at Fort William Henry comprised just over 2,000 men, half of whom were regulars, under the command of Lieutenant Colonel George Munro. The fort was a fairly strong structure, constructed of logs and earth. General Webb was stationed with 1,600 soldiers, mostly provincials, at Fort Edward, 22 km (14 miles) to the south. Webb dispatched a reinforcement of 200 regulars on 29 July to reinforce the garrison at Fort William Henry, and he also alerted the New York and New England colonies of the need for more troops. The message was received, but the reinforcements would arrive too late.

On 3 August, the first clashes occurred between scouts of the British and French armies. The road to Fort Edward was cut by a detachment of French and Indian troops, and British forces and civilians in the area began to withdraw to Fort William Henry, burning the houses and buildings that remained outside the perimeter. The British also held an entrenched camp outside the fort. British artillery fired upon the French build-up outside the fort, but the first French siege trenches were dug under heavy fire on the evening of 4 August and the siege began in earnest.

Both sides exchanged fire as the French trenches crept closer and closer to the British ramparts. A British artillery officer wrote on 7 August:

Robert Rogers. (John Carter Brown Library at Brown University)

the enemy still continue working and carrying on their approaches. The garrison kept a continual fire both of shells and cannon till night … [A]t night the garrison kept a continual watch for fear of an assault (8311-85).

Webb was unable to send more reinforcements, fearing that his small force would be decimated trying to reach the besieged British garrison. Such a loss would leave the road to Albany open and unprotected, since the provincial reinforcements had not yet arrived. To make matters worse, smallpox broke out inside Fort William Henry.

A few days into the siege, the number of killed and wounded within the fort had reached over 300. Many of the large British cannons and mortars had blown up or been destroyed. The palisades had been breached in a few locations, and the French continued to pour artillery fire into the fort. Messages sent by Munro had been intercepted by the French and Indians. Munro was advised of this state of affairs by Louis Antoine de Bougainville, a senior French officer, who warned that the likelihood of reinforcements from Webb was minimal. Munro still refused to surrender, but morale within the fort was sinking.

Following a full night of heavy bombardment Munro at last began to feel that resistance was futile. On the morning of 9 August, Lieutenant Colonel Young, was sent to Montcalm's tent to discuss terms of a surrender. The British agreed to a surrender that allowed them to march to Fort Edward with full military honors. They were also required to promise not serve in the conflict for 18 months. The French prisoners captured since 1754 were to be returned to New France within three months. The stores and artillery of the fort, or what was left of them, were retained as spoils of the French. Montcalm summoned a war council with his Indian allies and called on them to respect the conditions of the surrender. The British evacuated the fort and entrenched camp.

The French-allied Indians, disregarding Montcalm's demands, rushed to the fort as the British evacuated, attacking and killing the wounded left behind. The French guards attempted to stop the killing, but there is debate about how hard they tried. Montcalm was eventually able to restore some level of order, but on the following day, as the British column marched toward Fort Edward, they were attacked again by Indians seeking revenge and prisoners. The French guards again failed to stop the slaughter, and it is estimated that 50 men, women, and children were killed and another 200 taken prisoner by the Indians. The French finally managed to restore order and escort the remainder of the column to Fort Edward. Some of the Indians sickened and died of smallpox after their attacks on sick and wounded British.

By 11 August, the number of dead and wounded from the British side far exceeded the 300 who had been killed before the surrender of the fort and was well over 700 people killed, wounded, or missing. The French forces had lost fewer than 100 men killed and wounded. It is not known how many French-allied Indians died. However, a British prisoner of the Indians reported

that 'the Indians that went from the town [to Fort William Henry] where I lived one quarter of the numbers were missing, seven killed and three died of their wounds' (King). This suggests that the toll on some small Indian villages could have been quite high.

The partisan war on the frontier continued after the British defeat. Montcalm destroyed Fort William Henry and returned to Fort Carillon. He had been ordered to proceed to Fort Edward but had decided it was not a good idea, as the Canadian militia was nervous about getting back for the harvest. The year 1757 was the high water mark for the French effort in the French and Indian War; while the British were to suffer a few more defeats, the initiative began to shift in their favor with the 1758 campaign.

1758

One of the first major changes of 1758 was to the high command of British forces in North America, with the replacement of Lord Loudon by Major General James Abercromby. The Newcastle-Pitt Ministry also made concessions to the colonial governments on disputes over command and payment, in an effort to resolve past issues of reinforcements and supplies and make the way smoother for Abercromby. Britain agreed to pay for a portion of the raising, clothing, and arming of provincial units recruited for future campaigns, and to discontinue the custom of de-ranking provincial officers.

The British strategy for 1758 envisioned a large-scale, three-pronged attack on New France. Major General Abercromby was to lead an attack on Fort Carillon; Major General James Amherst was to lead an amphibious attack and siege of Louisbourg; and Brigadier John Forbes was to try once again to take Fort Duquesne, using a different route than Braddock had taken in 1755. Some 24,000 British regulars and 22,000 provincials were deployed for these campaigns, against a French force that was spread thinly across New France.

Western theater

Brigadier Forbes's expedition towards Fort Duquesne was different from Braddock's in several major ways. For a start the route was shorter and originated in Pennsylvania. Forbes also had a highly motivated and trained second-in-command, Lieutenant Colonel Henry Bouquet of the 60th Foot. Bouquet had been actively involved in drawing up battle plans and devising tactics to fight in the woods of North America. In 1757, he had drawn up a plan of marching in the woods that highlighted the need for a secure line of communications. His order of march focused on the need for constant scouting and destruction of any ambush, stating that

the vanguard must detach small parties a mile forward, who shall march in great silence, and visit all suspected places, as copses, ditches and hallows, where ambuscades may be concealed … [I]n case of attack, the men must fall on their knees; that motion will prevent their running away (Bouquet Papers I, pp. 52–53).

Forbes's march, though slow, was designed to ensure that forts were constructed and a secure line of communication ensured.

Forbes's expedition began to gather in Sandy Hook, Pennsylvania in April. The total number of troops earmarked for the column was about 6,000. Nearly 1,800 of these were regulars and the rest provincial soldiers. The period between April and June was spent gathering the necessary supplies and provincial troops for the operation. The issue of supplies was becoming acute; a press warrant was issued for the authorization of pressing wagons, carriages and horses if the situation did not improve by late May. This action was likely to be unpopular with colonial settlers and was used as a last resort.

The forward elements of the column began to move out in late June. On 24 June, Bouquet and forward elements reached Raystown, where they began to construct Fort Bedford. The troops would remain in the area for nearly a month, building the fort and securing the surrounding area. Forbes's division followed

and met up with the forward units. Bouquet then pushed out a further 64 km (40 miles) to Loyalhannon Creek and began to build up the road and another fortified position, Fort Ligonier. By 6 September, Bouquet and his forward elements were within 64 km (40 miles) of Fort Duquesne at Loyalhannon Creek. Forbes and his large force remained further back, hampered by discipline and supply problems. The onset of autumn rains delayed progress still further.

As they progressed along the march route, the British were also in negotiation with local Indian tribes. They wished particularly to win over the Delawares, who had sided with the French. After a series of meetings many of the Indian tribes agreed to side with the British, including some that had previously been allied with the French.

The French position at Fort Duquesne was still fairly formidable, even without a large contingent of regulars. Contemporary reports estimate that the fort was garrisoned by some 1,200 militia and marines, supported by an additional 1,000 Indian warriors, under the command of Marchand de Lignery.

It was at Loyalhannon Creek that Bouquet made a major operational error. Several British provincial and regular soldiers had been captured at Fort Ligonier by Indian raiding parties, and Bouquet was considering sending out two parties of 100 men each to cut off the Indian withdrawal and rescue the troops. Major Grant, a regular officer, suggested a different plan. He said that if Bouquet gave him 500–600 men, he would push towards Fort Duquesne, make a reconnaissance, attempt to cut off the roads and generally to harass the fort. British scouts had reported that the fort was garrisoned by only 600 men, so Bouquet agreed to the plan and Major Grant set out with a force of 400 regulars and 350 provincials.

Grant's force was within five miles of Fort Duquesne by 13 September, with a plan to destroy the Indian camp outside the fort. Major Lewis and a force of 400 men went forward and destroyed some of the blockhouses outside the fort, while Major Grant was stationed on a height overlooking

Battle of Fort William Henry, 1757

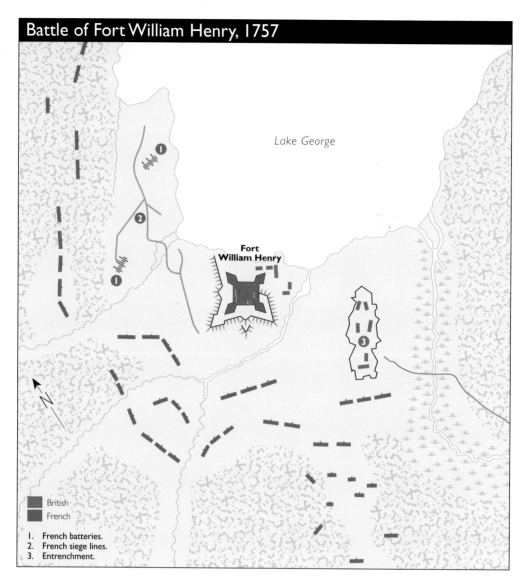

Lake George

Fort
William Henry

British
French

1. French batteries.
2. French siege lines.
3. Entrenchment.

the fort. When Lewis returned, Grant remained on the height. The following morning, 14 September, Grant divided his force into three columns. He sent Major Lewis to set up an ambush position with 100 regulars and 150 Virginian militia, while a Captain MacDonald marched to the fort with 100 regulars. Grant and the remainder of the force stayed on the heights.

As Grant reported to Bouquet, the execution of the plan went badly.

For about half an hour after the enemy came from the fort, in different parties, without much order and getting behind forces they advanced briskly, and attacked our left where there were 250 men. Captain MacDonald was soon killed … [O]ur people being overpowered, gave way, where those officers had been killed … [T]he 100 Pennsylvanians who were posted upon the right at the greatest distance from the enemy, went off without orders and without firing a shot. In short in less than half an hour all was in confusion … [W]e were fired upon from every quarter. … [O]rders were to no purpose, fear had then got the better of every other passion and I hope I shall never see again such pannick among troops (Bouquet papers, II, p. 503).

Braddock's and Forbes' routes, 1755–63

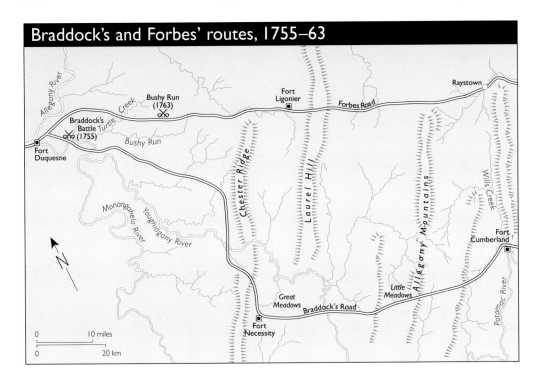

While the Pennsylvania provincials performed miserably, the Virginians acquitted themselves well. Bouquet noted: 'the Virginians who with 100 men sustained the battle with all their forces' (Bouquet, II, p. 519). In the end, Major Lewis and his detachment attempted to get back to Major Grant, but the two officers were forced to surrender to the French and Indians who had completely cut them off. More than 400 officers and men were able to escape, but some 200 had been killed or captured. It is difficult to ascertain accurate numbers of dead and wounded on the French side.

Following this victory, the French attempted to build on the advantage gained. In early October, 400 militia and marines and 100 Indians moved out to attack Fort Ligonier, arriving on the morning of 12 October. Bouquet was not in command at Fort Ligonier, having gone out on the road to make inspections. The French launched an attack at 11.00 am, pushing back two British forward reconnaissance units back toward the fort. The British commander, Colonel James Burd, counter-attacked, and after two hours of brisk fighting the French were forced to withdraw. Although this was a relatively minor skirmish for the French, morale at Fort Duquesne began to sink in the aftermath, and the French militia from Illinois and Louisiana withdrew. Supplies due from Fort Frontenac had been destroyed by Bradstreet in August, which was probably a contributing factor.

On 5 November, the main British force was finally established at Fort Ligonier. British scouts were reporting low morale at Fort Duquesne, and on 18 November 2,500 soldiers headed out from Fort Ligonier, hoping to exploit the situation. On the evening of 24 November, forward elements reached the heights where Grant had been stationed – just in time to witness the French blowing up their own fort. The next morning, the British moved into the remains of the fort and began to rebuild it, renaming it Fort Pitt. The campaign was a success, and the regulars were sent back to Philadelphia for winter quarters, while provincial troops stationed along the newly built road and its protecting forts.

New York theater

After spending the winter in Montreal, Montcalm decided to deploy most of his regular troops to Fort Carillon, and by early summer eight regular battalions were assembled there. They were largely without support from the Canadian militia, the vast majority of which was held back in Montreal, Quebec, and other frontier areas.

General Abercromby, in preparation for the attack on Fort Carillon, had assembled 6,000 British regulars and 9,000 provincials. The British column assembled at the ruins of Fort William Henry to drill and build bateaux for the lake crossing. On 4 July, the British force was completed and ready to sail.

Montcalm had realized that the British were on the move, and in early July he ordered his troops to build an outer defensive work around Fort Carillon. A large entrenchment was constructed, with felled trees spread out in front of the dug trenches. One British observer described how the '[French] had large cut trees one laid above another a man's height and in the outside there was brush and logs for about 15 paces from it' (Black Watch, p. 24). The British would have to overcome this obstacle before they could approach the fort itself.

The British force landed unopposed on the north shore of Lake George on 6 July. As they moved to the north on 7 July, a large-scale skirmish broke out on their left flank. The French were easily pushed aside by British light infantry and rangers, but in the fracas the innovative light infantry officer, Brigadier George Augustus, Lord Howe, was killed. A French senior officer Bouganville recorded the event: '[Howe] had showed the greatest talents. ... [The skirmish] gave us twenty-four hours delay' (Bougainville, p. 229). A British captain, Charles Lee, offers another reason for the delay of the British advance, claiming that 'our troops [were] a good deal scattered and divided through ignorance of the wood' (7803-18-1).

Colonel Bouquet meeting with Indians.
(Rare Book Division, New York Public Library)

After the skirmish, Montcalm gave orders for his troops to deploy to the entrenchment. Further work was done on the works in anticipation of the British attack, and seven of the eight battalions were stationed in the entrenchment. Only one battalion remained in Fort Carillon proper. Each battalion was allotted 130 paces of frontage. Montcalm was aware that there was not an endless supply of ammunition available to his army. He specifically ordered his officers to 'see to it the soldier fires slowly and they must urge him to take good aim' (Sautai, p. 72). On the morning of 8 July, the British were in sight of the entrenchment.

At this juncture, General Abercromby made the worst command decision possible. After a forward engineer party reported that the works should be attacked immediately, Abercromby decided to make a frontal attack without artillery support. This plan made no sense, even to his own officers. One British officer noted: '[entrenchment] made it impossible to force their breastworks without cannon' (*The Black Watch*, p. 24). Captain Lee was even more scathing: 'a miscarriage maybe brought about by the incapacity of a single person I really did not think that so great a share of stupidity and absurdity could be in possession of any man' (7803-18-1). At 10.00 am Bougainville commented: 'they [British] let off a great fusillade which did not interrupt our work at all; we amused ourselves by not replying' (Bougainville, p. 232).

Sources differ on what time the main British attack began, but it was most likely sometime around 12.00 pm. Bougainville described how four main British columns attacked the entrenchment. Another French officer noted: 'our musketry fire was so well aimed that the enemy was destroyed as soon as they appeared' (Sautai, p. 77). While the British attacks were not immediately destroyed, they suffered heavy casualties as recorded by an officer of the 42nd Foot: 'had as hot a fire for about three hours as possibly could be, we all the time seeing but their hats and end of their muskets' (Black Watch, p. 24).

There are estimated to have been six major British attacks throughout the day, without a single successful breach of the breastwork. Montcalm commented that 'every part of the entrenchment was successively attacked with the greatest vigour' (Sautai, p. 85), while Charles Lee described 'attacks made with most perfect regularity, coolness and resolution' (7803-18-1). French grenadier and light companies were shifted to dangerous holes in the defense. Bougainville told of: 'their [British] light troops and better marksmen, who, protected by the trees, delivered a most murderous fire on us' (Bougainville, p. 232).

Captain Lee summarized the reasons for the defeat with his account of how the unevenness and ruggedness of the ground and height of the breastwork

> ... rendered it an absolute impossibility ... [N]o order given to change attack ... but every officer led at the head of his division, company or squadron to fall a sacrifice to his own good behaviour and stupidity of his commander [Abercromby] ... [T]he fire was prodigiously hot and the slaughter of the officers was great; almost all wounded, the men still furiously rushing forward almost without leaders, five hours persisted in this diabolical attempt and at length obliged to retire (7803-18-1).

At about 7.00 pm the British began to withdraw towards Lake George. Some of the troops, after suffering such a setback, became demoralized, and Captain Bradstreet was ordered to march back to the landing place and ensure that no one stole or seized the boats. The light infantry and rangers protected the retreat as the boats were loaded, and the remaining elements of the expedition withdrew to the south end of Lake George. From there the retreat continued to Fort Edward.

The battle casualties for British were more than 1,000 regulars and 300 provincials killed. The French, by contrast, lost only 300 killed in the battle. General Abercromby's demonstration of poor leadership and decision-making skills, contrasted against Major General Jeffrey Amherst's success at Louisbourg (see below), led shortly to Abercromby's replacement as commander-in-chief by Amherst in September.

There was one bright spot in the conduct of the New York campaign. Captain Bradstreet, a regular officer, led a raid with a small waterborne force against Fort Frontenac in August. His force of 2,200 men was made up mostly of provincial soldiers, with about 500 regulars among them. Bradstreet and his men traveled by bateaux up the Mohawk and Onandaga rivers past Oswego. On 22 August, the force left Oswego and sailed due north for Fort Frontenac.

On 25 August, the flotilla arrived near Frontenac. The French garrison had been depleted in response to the need for regulars at Fort Carillon, and on 27 August, the fort and French shipping in the region were under bombardment by British artillery. The fort surrendered later the same day. Nine French ships, as well as the fort, were destroyed in the attack, and the booty gained from seizing this important trading post and its supplies was estimated to have been close to 800,000 pounds sterling. Just as important, seizing the supplies and stores from Fort Frontenac caused major problems for the French forts in the west.

Canadian theater

The major engagement in the Canadian theater took place on Cape Breton Island, home of the French fort at Louisbourg. This structure was the strongest fortress in North America, for either side, with defenses stretching for a mile and a half on its landward perimeter. Some of the masonry was in a poor condition owing to the weather conditions of the area, which would prove beneficial to the British artillery. Defensive lines had been dug along the beaches to the south and west of the fortress, and four bastions stood within the fort itself. The governor of Cape Breton Island, Chevalier de Drucour, was in overall command of the French forces at Louisbourg. There were four battalions of regulars, 24 companies of marines, and some militia. Contemporary accounts estimate that there were 3,500 men stationed in and around the fortress. There

Battle of Fort Carillon showing the entrenchment with no felled trees in front. (National Archives of Canada)

were 219 cannons on the fortress walls and other defensive positions, as well as 19 mortars. The garrison was prepared for a long siege. A French fleet had arrived over the course of the spring to re-supply the fortress. Five ships of the line and seven frigates patrolled the harbor.

The British forces were gathered at Halifax, Nova Scotia. The Royal Navy had provided 23 ships of the line, 18 frigates and a fleet of transports, under the command of Admiral Edward Boscawen. Major General Jeffrey Amherst, was to lead the land effort. Once again, as in 1757, the expedition was made up mostly of regulars. There were 14 regular battalions earmarked for the operation, comprising just over 12,000 men with an additional 500 'Gorham's Rangers' from Halifax and Royal Artillery attached. The fleet sailed on 28 May, and arrived off the Cape Breton coast on 2 June.

There were three possible landing sites. The first was Freshwater Cove, 6 km (four miles) from the fort. Flat Point and White Point were to the east of Freshwater, closer to the fort. Royal Navy and senior army officers sailed up and down the potential landing areas to assess the best approach, then devised their plans. The army was to be divided into three divisions: Brigadier James Wolfe was to lead the main assault against Freshwater Cove, with Brigadiers Charles Lawrence and Edward Whitmore advancing towards Flat and White Points.

The fleet and army were delayed from landing for more than six days, as fog and surf denied access to the beaches. The French defenses were strongest at Freshwater Cove, where their entrenchment was ready to receive the enemy. Over 1,000 French soldiers had been deployed to throw the British back into the sea and were, as a British officer noted:

most advantageously posted behind good entrenchment, the banks very high and almost perpendicular … [W]herever there was the least probability of getting ashore it was well secured with cannon and entrenchment (7204-6-2).

Finally, on 8 June, the troops received the order to land. A British observer described 'nothing seen or heard for one hour but the thundering of Cannon and flashes of lightening' (Add Mss 45662). Wolfe's division was to see most of the heavy fighting for the day. The surf continued to be a problem – 'the surge was extremely violent … [Boats] crushed to pieces being carried away by the surf' (6807-131).

The first waves of British troops approached the beaches. An officer who landed with Wolfe's division noted:

the boats proceeded to the cove, the enemy let them come within half musket shot and gave them a warm reception from their entrenchment, with great guns and small arms (Military Affairs, p. 416).

As Wolfe's division made a foothold at Freshwater Cove, Lawrence's division also landed after making a diversion. The French were overwhelmed by the numbers of British troops landing, and began to fear that they were in danger of being cut off from the fort. A British officer recorded the attack:

the enemy's attention being quite engaged at the other cove did not perceive our men climbing rocks till a few of them got to the top who bravely maintained their guard well supported though opposed by numbers they gained the enemy's flank who feared being cut off from the garrison fled in great disorder (7204-6-2).

Each side lost about 100 men during the fight for the beaches.

Flat Point Cove became the landing place for the British artillery and stores, once the area had been secured by the troops moving from Freshwater, and a camp was built to receive troops and materiel coming ashore. General Amherst decided that the best way to deal with the fort was to surround it with batteries and slowly pummel it into submission. A formal European-style siege was planned; unlike Abercromby, Amherst decided against a frontal infantry attack.

Montcalm cheered by his men after his victory at Fort Carillon, 1758. (Fort Ticonderoga Museum)

On 12 June, Brigadier Wolfe and 2,000 men set out to seize Lighthouse battery, to the north of the fort. The British had received reports that the French had destroyed Lighthouse and Great Battery, two of the major batteries outside Louisbourg's walls. A French officer stated the reason for abandoning the batteries: 'the impossibility of maintaining this post obliged us to abandon it; for it was more than we could do to guard the batteries and ramparts of the city' (Knox, III, p. 104). Wolfe's forces reached the abandoned lighthouse battery on 20 June. They took possession and immediately opened fire on French shipping in the harbor and other French positions close by. The Island battery, opposite Louisbourg, was silenced on 25 June when the combined artillery fire from the Lighthouse and Royal Navy ships finally destroyed the will of the defenders.

On 29 June, the French sank six ships in the entrance to the harbor to deny access to the Royal Navy. Louisbourg was now completely surrounded and closed off to the outside world. The formal siege had begun. The British deployed infantry to various redoubts, set up siege batteries, and began to dig siege trenches towards the fortress.

The outcome of the siege was decided by the ability of the engineers and artillery men on both sides. The French did not sit idly in the fortress under the onslaught of British artillery. One French officer described a typical series of actions:

1st of July a detachment of our people sallied out of the wood ... [T]here was a very brisk skirmish, but at length our men were forced to retire ... [W]e made a sally on the 8th ... [W]e surprised them ... but what could 900 men do against the vanguard of the enemy who immediately flew to assistance of the sappers (Knox, III, p. 110).

Battle at Fort Carillon, 1758

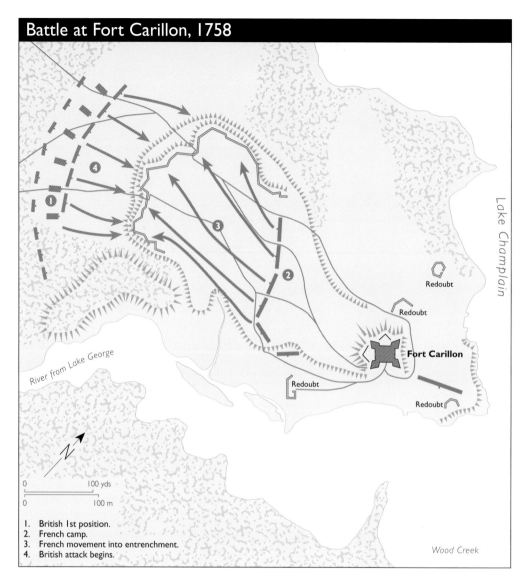

1. British 1st position.
2. French camp.
3. French movement into entrenchment.
4. British attack begins.

The siege was dangerous as well for the British soldiers out in the redoubts and trenches. A British officer described what befell an overly curious fellow officer: '[a] cannon ball which cut his head off as he looked over the breastwork out of curiosity not duty' (8001-30).

By late July, the French defenders were beginning to suffer the effects of the siege in earnest. The British siege lines were continuing to close in, and a French 63-gun ship of the line had been destroyed in the harbor. A French officer described the conditions of the French batteries:

as our batteries and ramparts had been very much damaged these three days, and as the fire of the enemy's small arms made it almost impracticable for us to maintain ourselves on those ramparts which we were endeavouring to repair … a breach had been [made] in the Dauphin Bastion and West Gate (Knox, III, p. 112).

He continued 'in so melancholy a situation, there was nothing left but to capitulate; so that we suspended our fire, and sent to demand a truce, in order to regulate the articles of surrender' (Knox, III, p. 113). The French garrison surrendered on 26 July.

Lieutenant General Jeffrey Amherst. (Ann Ronan Picture Library)

The British had lost 500 killed and 1,000 wounded during the landings and the siege. The French losses are estimated at 1,000 killed and 2,000 wounded. More than 5,000 soldiers, sailors, and civilians surrendered to the British forces. The siege had taken most of the 1758 campaign season, however, and the advance towards Quebec City would have to wait until the following year. A large garrison was left at Louisbourg to rebuild the works and defend the area against potential French counter attacks. The remainder of the troops were transported to Halifax and New York for winter quarters.

The campaigns of 1758 had definitively shifted the momentum of the war in Great Britain's favor. New France was now completely on the defensive. While Abercromby had been stopped at Fort Carillon, it was only a matter of time before the British attacked it again with a different operational plan.

1759

Given their successes the previous year, the British decided once again to adopt a multi-pronged strategy for the 1759 campaign. The major thrust, against Quebec City, would be commanded by Major General James Wolfe. Wolfe's force was almost completely composed of regular troops; he had 10 battalions, plus a composite unit of grenadiers named the 'Louisbourg Grenadiers'. A small force of 300 provincial engineers and six companies of Rangers joined the force. The total number was just over 8,000 men. The force was smaller than the one that had attacked Louisbourg, since a garrison was required to remain at the Fort in case of French naval counterattacks. General Amherst was to lead a mixed force of provincials and regulars against Fort Carillon and Fort St. Frederic, with Montreal as his final objective. Amherst's force numbered just over 5,800 regulars and 5,000 provincials. A third pincer, commanded by Brigadier John Prideaux, was to originate from the re-established Fort Oswego and strike towards Fort Niagara. Prideaux' force included three battalions of regulars and two battalions of provincials. The last campaign was to be carried out by a very small force, ordered to reopen communications between Fort Pitt and Fort Ligonier, and then to establish a force at Fort Pitt to attack north against Forts Presque Isle and Venango.

Western theater
The regulars of 1/60th Foot marched from Lancaster, Pennsylvania on 31 May. After a month of undertaking repairs and ensuring security along the road, the battalion arrived at Fort Bedford. They spent June and early July carrying supplies and reinforcements to Fort Pitt, amid much skirmishing.

The 1/60th Foot received orders to march from Fort Pitt toward Fort Venango on 12 July. As the troops moved out, they received news that the French had abandoned both Venango and Presque Isle, as well as several other nearby posts, after receiving news of the fall of Fort Niagara to British troops. The 1/60th marched out to search the forts, and confirmed that they had been abandoned. The regulars returned to Fort Pitt, while provincial troops were deployed north to occupy the forts for the winter. Five companies of the 1/60th Foot remained at Fort Pitt for the winter, so that they would be in a position to move quickly if the frontier was threatened. The rest of the battalion was sent along the road to Lancaster to keep the lines of communications open for the winter.

New York theater

In March 1759, General Amherst ordered a large-scale raid on Fort Carillon. A mixed force of regulars, rangers, and Indians was ordered to observe the French and the area around Fort Carillon to assess its defenses. The raiding party destroyed French supplies outside the fort, captured five French

soldiers, and drew accurate maps of the defenses of the fort and the entrenchment, losing two men in the process.

General Amherst gathered his forces on the southern end of Lake George over the course of June. While stationed there, the forces were drilled and trained for the coming operation. A contemporary account described preparations:

the regular regiments of line will be ready formed at the head of their encampment, between four and five o'clock to-morrow morning, if a fine day, the men to be in their

waistcoats with their arms and ammunition (Knox, II, p. 486).

Amherst built part of a fort at the entrenchment constructed in 1757 and named it Fort George. He also ensured that forts were constructed between Fort Edward and Fort George to protect his rear in case a French attack originated from behind. He waited throughout June and most of July for sufficient reinforcements to arrive for his regulars and for the provincial forces to be fully mustered. On 21 July the army entered bateaux and began to sail north. They arrived at the northern end of the lake on 22 July and began to advance towards Fort Carillon.

Chevalier de Bourlamaque had reinforced Fort Carillon with 3,000 regulars and 1,000 militia troops in mid-May. However, he then received information that the British were planning to land near Quebec, only with orders to withdraw his forces from Carillon and attempt to hold the line at the north end of Lake Champlain. Nevertheless, he decided to hamper the approaching British before he withdrew.

A small but powerful French force of 400 men was left at Fort Carillon to repel the British approach. Bourlamaque decided to withdraw north to Fort St. Frederic following reports that Amherst's column was marching on the fort. The French force at Fort Carillon held up Amherst's force with artillery fire for four days, until Amherst moved his heavy artillery into range and began to pound the fort. Amherst noted on 26 July that

the artillery will be up that we may open batteries of six 24 pounders … [A]t about 10 PM a deserter came in and said the garrison was to get off and blow up the fort … and soon we saw the fort on fire and an explosion (Jeffrey Amherst, 26/7/1759).

The French force withdrew from Fort Carillon to meet up with Bourlamaque and his forces. The French decided to blow up

British amphibious landings at Louisbourg. The landing has a mix of British line and grenadier troops. (Aisa)

Halifax, Nova Scotia, the main staging area for the conquest of Louisbourg and Quebec. (National Archives of Canada)

Fort St. Frederic a few days later, fearing that it could not withstand the powerful British artillery train which was fast approaching. Bourlamaque and his troops then withdrew to Isle-aux-Noix.

Amherst decided against continuing his advance on the French immediately. He decided to take some time to fortify Fort Carillon, renamed Fort Ticonderoga, and Fort St. Frederic, now Crown Point. Amherst also sent Robert Rogers and his Rangers on a long-distance raid to destroy the Indian village of St. Francis. His scouts and rangers also sailed north from Crown Point to the northern end of Lake Champlain to observe and assess French preparations for defense. Troops were further engaged in building more bateaux and other shipping, to contend with the small French

flotilla of armed whaleboats on the lake. Amherst did not attempt to resume the northward march until 11 October.

After an unsuccessful attempt to destroy the French shipping, on 19 October Amherst decided to withdraw for the winter to Crown Point and Fort Ticonderoga. The advance north on Lake Champlain, to the St. Jean River to deal with the forts outside Montreal, would have to wait until the next campaign season, but the French presence on Lake George and the southern areas of Lake Champlain had been destroyed.

The other major offensive in the New York theater was launched against Fort Niagara. As mentioned previously, Brigadier Prideaux commanded three regular and two provincial battalions. By early spring, the forward elements of his column had reached Oswego, and began work to fortify the area for future operations.

Captain M. Pouchot commanded the French garrison at Fort Niagara. His troops

Siege of Louisbourg

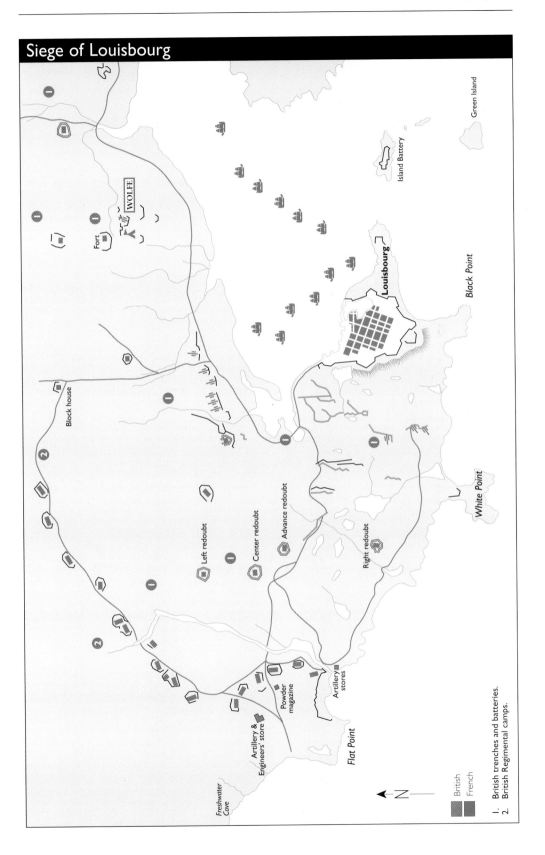

British trenches and batteries.
British Regimental camps.

British
French

1. British trenches and batteries.
2. British Regimental camps.

numbered 110 men from regular battalions, 180 Marines, and 100 Canadian militia. The fortifications at Niagara were quite good, however, and when Pouchot received word of the British arrival at Oswego, he set about repairing damage to the fort from weather and made other improvements to prepare for the inevitable British attack.

The British force was divided at Oswego. Eight regular companies of the 4/60th Foot and one battalion of New York Provincials remained to defend Oswego and complete work on a new fort. Two companies of the 4/60th Foot, along with the 44th and 46th Foot and one battalion of New York provincials, sailed for Fort Niagara in early July. They arrived near the fort on 7 July, and immediately prepared to lay siege. Skirmishes with the French were frequent as the British advanced.

By 16 July, the British had closed off all routes into Fort Niagara except for the water approaches. The formal siege began as both sides opened fire with artillery. The British, using trenches, moved steadily closer to the walls. Prideaux was accidentally killed by one of his own mortars during an artillery exchange, and Colonel William Johnson assumed command. He immediately called for further reinforcements from Oswego, following reports from scouts of a rumor that a French relieving force was on the march from Presque Isle and Venango.

On 24 July, the French force appeared from the south and the two sides met at La Belle Famille. There were 800 French troops present, and Johnson had deployed just over 400 regulars. The British, however, managed to surprise the French as they came within firing range. As was often the case in battles of the 18th century, the French lost any advantage their numerical superiority might have given them, when the British were able to fire into their column as they attempted to deploy into linear formation. Jeffrey Amherst noted 'Johnson had intelligence of their [French] approach and dispersed his people [so] that he beat and routed them, [and] took 160 prisoners'

(Jeffrey Amherst, p. 151). The commander of the British force, Lieutenant Colonel Eyre Massy, commented: 'The men received the enemy with vast resolution, and never fired one shot, until we could almost reach them with our bayonets' (Brumwell, p. 253).

On 25 July, Pouchot ordered a raiding party of 150 men to attack the British trenches. The attack failed, and on 26 July, the French surrendered the fort. The survivors from the battle of La Belle Famille had already withdrawn towards Fort Detroit in the west, and the surrender of Fort Niagara effectively destroyed the French presence on the western frontier. Any threat to Fort Pitt had already been removed when the forts at Presque Isle and Venango were abandoned.

Canadian theater

In May 1759, Montcalm learned that a sizeable British fleet was heading towards Quebec City from Louisbourg. Until this news was received, many in the French command had expected that the attack would come from the Lake Champlain region. The St. Lawrence River was widely considered too difficult for a full fleet to navigate. However, unknown to the French, a young Royal Navy officer, James Cook, had surveyed the St. Lawrence, giving the British the information they needed to stage a waterborne assault. Units of militia and Indians were called to Quebec to bolster the French defense, and by late May 14,000 men had been deployed to defend Quebec. These included five regular battalions, most of the Marines for New France, and militia units. A French observer described preparations:

all along the [St. Lawrence] coast as far as Montmorency Falls, redoubts, bastions and batteries were placed at a distance of a gunshot from one another, and here M. de Montcalm placed his whole army (Northcliffe Collection, p. 215).

The French regulars were stationed in the center with militia and a stiffening of marines to their left and right. The gates of

Major General James Wolfe (Roger-Viollet)

Quebec City were heavily barricaded and more than 100 artillery pieces put in place.

The British force, as mentioned previously, numbered just under 9,000 men. (French intelligence reports had consistently overestimated the actual size of the fleet.) On 21 June, the British fleet was first sighted from Quebec. After a series of reconnaissance and surveying missions, the fleet landed the British force on Isle d'Orleans on 26 June. The British troops were able to land unopposed, opposite the French lines at Beauport. Montcalm ordered fire ships to be deployed against the British anchorage, but, as an eyewitness noted, 'fire-ships were sent down to burn enemy shipping, but, instead of doing it, what was our surprise to see the fire ships ablaze two leagues away' (Northcliffe Collection, p. 216). On the evening of 29 June, a British brigade under the command of Brigadier Robert Monckton landed at Point Levi, opposite Quebec City. The brigade had cleared the area and heights by 30 June, and by 12 July had established batteries to fire on Quebec City.

The two remaining brigades, under the command of Brigadiers James Murray and George Townshend, landed opposite the left flank of the French positions stationed at Montmorency Falls on 10 July. Wolfe had decided to attempt to turn the French left flank at some point. Montcalm did not move across the Montmorency to attack Wolfe's new camp. Wolfe sent out skirmishing parties in an attempt to force Montcalm into attacking him across the river, but Montcalm did not move.

Wolfe decided to make a combined amphibious attack from the St. Lawrence and across the Montmorency River against the French left flank at Montmorency Falls. On the morning of 31 July, the Royal Navy began to bombard the Montmorency positions. This alerted the French to the possibility of a major attack, and Montcalm reinforced this position with men from the center and right flank. The landing did not take place until 5.00 pm on the 31st, when the British landed the 'Louisbourg

Grenadiers' and elements of the 60th Foot from the St. Lawrence. These troops were earmarked to seize two redoubts, the first of which was speedily completed. Reinforcements from two other regiments were then landed. What happened next destroyed any hope of a British victory. Accounts vary of exactly what happened and who was responsible, but it appears that the grenadiers rushed forward and seized a redoubt at the base of the hill, without having received orders to do so. This action undermined the British commanders' plan to launch a combined attack. A sergeant-major of the grenadiers recalled:

we fixed our bayonets and beat our grenadiers march and so advanced on, during all this time their cannon played very briskly on us, but their small arms in their trenches lay cool till they were sure of their mark then poured their small shot like showers of hail, which caused our brave grenadiers to fall very fast (Journal of a Sergeant Major, p. 10).

Other observers were more critical of the grenadiers' actions. A junior officer. Lieutenant Hamilton commented:

[t]he check the grenadiers met with yesterday will it is hoped be a diffusion to them for the future. They ought to know that such impetuous, irregular, un-soldierlike behaviour destroys all order and makes it impossible for their commanders to form any disposition for an attack and puts it out of the general's power to execute his plans ... [T]he very first fire of the enemy was sufficient to repulse men who had lost all sense of order and military discipline (6707-11).

James Wolfe recorded his thoughts: 'the grenadiers landed ... their disorderly march and strange behaviour necessity of calling them off and desisting from the attack ... [M]any experienced officers hurt in this foolish business' (Wolfe, 31 July). A French observer noted that '[Montcalm] allowed the enemy to advance within easy musket range, when he ordered his army to fire'.

Fort Niagara, 1759

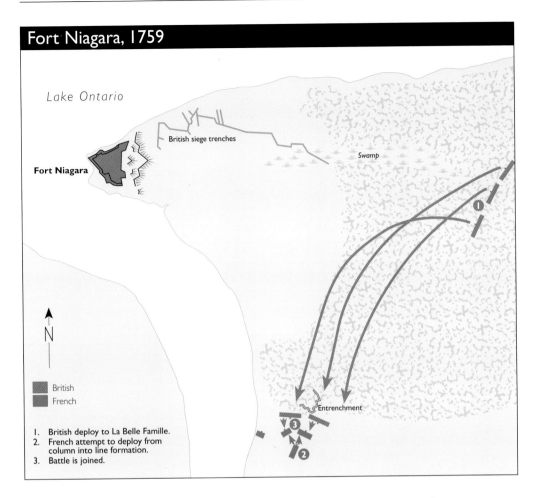

Lake Ontario

British siege trenches

Fort Niagara

Swamp

N

British
French

1. British deploy to La Belle Famille.
2. French attempt to deploy from column into line formation.
3. Battle is joined.

Entrenchment

(Northcliffe, p. 218). The outcome of the engagement was succinctly conveyed by Marquis de Bougainville: 'the enemy was repulsed with a loss of six or seven hundred men, and in the retreating they burned two of their anchored vessels' (Bougainville, p. 318). In the end the estimate of British casualties was just over 400 killed and wounded.

The French did not follow up the British withdrawal, and the British were able to leave unmolested. The main French army had not been destroyed, however, which enormously frustrated Wolfe. He continued to send detachments of light infantry, Indians, and rangers out to destroy French villages in an attempt to draw Montcalm out of his entrenchment and into open battle. As he stated on 7 August, 'large detachments sent to scour the woods

and to oblige the enemy to keep at a distance and to prepare the troops for a decisive action' (Wolfe, 7 August). He was unsuccessful in provoking Montcalm throughout the month of August. A British officer noted: 'the next attempt [post-Montmorency] will, I hope, be more practicable and more successful; if we can't beat them we shall ruin their country' (Pargellis, Military Affairs, p. 434). On 9 and 10 August, a British attempt to draw battle was sent against the French positions at Point aux Trembles. As with Montmorency, these attacks failed. The French positions were very strong, and an observer described the engagement thus: 'their loss was 100 men killed and wounded the first time, and 250 the second. Our side lost two men killed and 4 or 5 wounded' (Northcliffe, p. 219).

Quebec: Direct View. (Roger-Viollet)

By early September, Wolfe felt pressure to bring the campaign to a decisive end. Autumn was approaching and the harsh Canadian winter would put a stop to the campaign, but bring no resolution. If the British withdrew it would be a major blow to morale and to the campaign in North America. Wolfe decided to take a gamble; on 6 September, he embarked five battalions on Royal Navy transports and ships and sailed up the St. Lawrence to the bottom of the bluffs below Quebec City. Testing the resolve of Montcalm to counter his aggression, his ships sailed up and down the river, making surveys of possible landing sites, until 11 September. On 12 September, he re-embarked a division of troops and sailed for the lower end of the river. Wolfe had decided on a specific point below the cliffs which led to a large plain, known as the Plains of Abraham, which stood to the west of the city. There is some controversy as to how Wolfe gained the necessary information; some sources say that Wolfe had gathered the information himself, while others claim that a French deserter pointed out the potential weak spot in the fort's defenses.

Brigadier Townsend describes what happened next in his report of the evening and morning of 13 September:

light infantry scramble up a woody precipice in order to secure ye landing of the troops by dislodging a Captains Guard, defending a small intrenched road ye troops were to move up. After a little firing ye light infantry gained the top of the Precipice and dispersed the Captain's Guard ... by which means the troops... soon got up and were immediately formed. The boats as they emptied were sent back directly for the second disembarkation, which I immediately made ... General Wolfe thereupon began to form his army (Northcliffe, p. 419).

Montcalm thought that Wolfe's landing was a trick. A British observer recorded that 'the Marquis de Montcalm when he heard the British had ascended the hill still believed it to be a feint' (Add Mss 45662). He realized his mistake when the

British began to take to the field. Montcalm moved as many troops as he could over to Quebec in an attempt to destroy the British landing and positions that were being drawn up. The armies were in sight of one another, and Wolfe at last had the decisive battle that had eluded him since June.

Although there were periods of North American-style skirmishing throughout the battle, it was mostly fought in conventional style, with linear formations deciding the outcome. A British junior officer gives incredible detail of the developments of 13 September, describing how the British formed lines

... about two miles from Quebec. Here we lay on our arms and were very much annoyed by some Canadians who from behind the hills and from a thicket on our left kept a most galling fire ... [A]t about 9am the enemy [French] had drawn up ... [They] advanced towards us briskly and in good order. We stood to receive them. They began fire at too great a distance ... as they came nearer fired on them by divisions ... [F]ire made them waiver a bit ... [H]owever they still advanced pretty quick. We increased our fire without altering our position. When they were 60 yards gave them a full fire, fixed bayonets and under cover of smoke pushed at them. When they perceived us they immediately turned their backs and fled (7204-6-2).

A British Sergeant-Major recalled: 'in about a quarter of an hour the enemy gave way on all sides, when a terrible slaughter ensued from the quick Fire of our field guns and musketry,

Quebec campaign, 1759

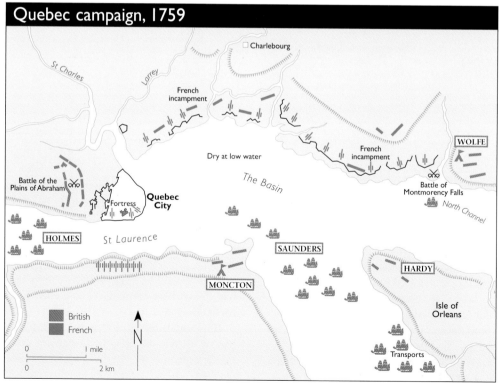

Attack at Montmorency Falls. In the foreground, the Royal Navy ships can clearly be seen giving fire support to the troops on the beaches. In the distance are British artillery firing at Quebec from the south bank of the river. (National Archives of Canada)

with which we pursued them to the walls of the town' (Sergent Major, p. 22). The British lost 50 men killed, including Wolfe, who died of gunshot wounds, and 500 wounded. The French lost more than 1,500 killed, wounded, and taken prisoner. Montcalm was mortally wounded, and died on 14 September in the city.

The battle for control of the city and fortress was far from over. The town and fortress had still not been taken, and the British began to build a camp to lay siege to the town. Reinforcements and artillery were brought over from Point Levis. Marquis de Bougainville and a large part of the French force had not yet been engaged. He reported:

I was not informed of it [arrival of British troops on the Plains of Abraham] until nine in the morning. I marched at once, but when I came within range of the battle, our army was beaten and in retreat. The entire English Army advanced to attack me. I retreated before them and posted myself so as to cover the retreat of our army, or join with it, or to march again against the enemy if it was judged proper ... On the 18th I marched with six hundred men to throw myself into Quebec ... I was only three quarters of a league from Quebec when I learned that the city had surrendered. It had been bombarded for sixty-eight days ... [W]e spent three months in bivouac. Just the same, the English hold only the outer walls and the King [Louis XV] still holds the colony (Bougainville, pp.320-1).

While the British had been very successful in 1759, the French still had a large force stationed outside Quebec and in Montreal. The momentum that had shifted to the British in 1758 continued in 1759, but the French remained defiant in the face of defeat. The British were surrounded at Quebec. Winter was coming and the

British volunteers scaling the cliffs below the Plains of Abraham. (National Archives of Canada)

St. Lawrence would freeze, preventing the Royal Navy from delivering supplies. A major reinforcement of troops and materiel was required to contend with the encroaching French forces, and then to march to Montreal to take on the French units remaining there. The Battle of the Plains of Abraham was a critical turning point in the campaign, but it did not end the conflict. As a British observer, Lieutenant Williamson, noted: 'we are masters of the capital its true but it does not follow from thence that we have conquered the whole country, that entirely depends on our fleet' (7311-85). A second battle outside Quebec and a campaign against Montreal would need to be won before the British could claim victory in North America.

1760

The fighting in 1760 was marked by two major engagements: the second Battle of the Plains of Abraham (also known as Sainte-Foy) and the British offensive against the last remaining French post, Montreal. This section will look first at the Canadian theater of operations as this was the first, and most significant, campaign of 1760.

Canadian theater

The British garrison left in Quebec City spent the winter months in a virtual state of siege. They were holed up in the city and a few surrounding positions in the countryside, closed off from the outside world by the frozen St. Lawrence River. During the winter the British suffered due to the lack of proper winter housing. As a British observer noted: 'during the whole siege from first to last, 535 houses were burnt down, among [them] the whole eastern part of the lower town' (Sergeant-Major, p. 24). It was estimated that by March 1760, half of the garrison force was on the sick list due to scurvy

and illnesses aggravated by the weather conditions. The British, under the command of Major General Murray, were also forced to send forage parties outside the city walls to

supplement their supplies. These parties
were regularly attacked by rear guards of the
French forces. During the winter of
1759–60, the British constantly anticipated

the arrival of a large French force from
Montreal. Rumors circulated for months
that the French, under the command of
Marquis de Levis, were about to march on

Quebec, creating a sense of urgency to prepare for the worst.

The French, meanwhile, had quartered some of their regulars in Montreal, as well as in outposts near Quebec. The militia had been dismissed, ready to be called up again for duty in the spring of 1760. The French decided to attack Quebec before the ice on the St. Lawrence had broken up and the British could get reinforcements. By mid-March, orders were received to gather supplies and prepare for the march to the north, and the militia was called out once again. On 20 April, the French forces began to march. The column numbered more than 6,000 men, comprising eight regular battalions, 20 Marine companies, 3,000 militia, and 400 Indians. As the force marched north, various detachments were called in and the number rose to over 8,000 effectives.

The British received reports of a French column approaching from Montreal. One British observer recalled that 'during ye night of the 26th and 27th [a soldier] brought certain intelligence that the French were in motion to come by ye way of Lorette and St. Foy to cut off our Camp Rouge posts' (Northcliffe, p. 427). Bougainville also commented that 'the speed of [Levis'] march surprised the enemy' (Bougainville, p. 325). The French drove off any British light troops they encountered and began to build a camp at Sainte-Foy, at the western edge of the Plains of Abraham. General Murray made a critical mistake at this point; instead of assessing the situation and numbers of French forces, he decided to advance out of the city and prepare an entrenchment. He could have waited behind the walls of the city until the ice broke up and a reliving force had arrived. Instead, as one British officer, captain Knox recalled, 'about seven o'clock our army marched out to the Heights of Abraham with a respectable artillery' (Knox Journal, p. 246). A French observer, J. Desbruyeres, described '[Murray's] garrison consisting of

3,000 men ... the numbers of French appearing but small their brigades being then sheltered by the woods' (Northcliffe, p. 427).

The 10 British battalions were drawn up on the heights and as the French army was in disorder they moved to attack. The French began to deploy from column into line as the British approached. The first volleys occurred on the British right and French left flank between forward units. British light infantry engaged and

Death of James Wolfe. (National Archives of Canada)

defeated a large group of French grenadiers. British rangers engaged French advanced troops on the French right and again the French were defeated. However, the main French force arrived at this stage and overwhelmed the British light infantry, forcing them to withdraw. They then turned their attention to the British right wing, followed by an attack on the British left flank. The French began to outflank the British line, in an attempt to get between them and the city.

The British artillery was of little use because the main battle line had shifted forward. A British officer lamented that 'our cannon were of no service to us as we could not draw them through the soft ground and gulleys of snow 3 feet deep' (7204-6-2). It was during this heavy fighting that Murray realized at last how much danger his troops were in, and ordered a withdrawal to the city. The British, supported by heavy fire into the French lines, were able to retreat in good order.

Death of Montcalm. (National Archives of Canada)

Knox reported that 'this discomfirt
[withdrawal] was however so regularly
conducted that the enemy did
not pursue with the spirit which the vast
importance of their victory required'
(Knox, Journal, p. 248).

The battle had lasted just over two
hours. One-third of the British force had
been killed, wounded, or captured, while
the French had lost 2,000 men. By 29 April,
the French were within 600 yards of the
city and began to build trenches and siege
batteries to pound the city into submission.
The British responded by further reinforcing
their own batteries and positions. As
Bougainville noted, the deciding factor
during the siege was not Levis' troops
and artillery; 'the arrival of an English
squadron decided the matter, it was
necessary to raise the siege' (Bougainville,
p. 325). On 15 May, the Royal Navy arrived

to lift the siege of Quebec. The French withdrew, except for a small force ordered to shadow the British movements from Quebec to Montreal.

Advance on Montreal

General Amherst decided to attack Montreal with another multi-pronged movement. After Murray and his troops had been re-supplied and reformed in Quebec, he was ordered to advance down the St. Lawrence from the northeast. On 2 July, Murray and 2,400 regulars embarked for Montreal, followed by a reinforcement of just over 1,000 men from Louisbourg. The second prong, under the command of Brigadier William de Haviland, was to march with 3,400 regulars, provincials, and Indians from Lake Champlain up the St. John River and then north-west towards Montreal. De Haviland began his march in August. The

Ruins of Quebec after the siege of 1759. (National Archives of Canada)

third prong and largest force was to be under the command of General Amherst himself. Amherst, with a force of 10,000 regulars and provincials, planned to launch an attack from Fort Oswego and then Fort Frontenac up the St. Lawrence to attack Montreal from the west. He began his advance on 10 August.

Murray's force should have had to contend with French forces at Trois Rivieres, but he decided to avoid the 2,000 troops stationed there. He bypassed Trois Rivieres altogether and sailed for Montreal, landing just north at Sorel. The French forces in the area were gathering to destroy his force, but Murray sent out rangers and other units with proclamations for the militia to lay down their arms, which many did, after hearing reports that those who refused to surrender were being burned out of their houses. By the end of August most of the French forces opposing Murray had gone home.

De Haviland successfully cut off Bougainville's force of 1,000 from their lines of communication with St. Jean and

Marquis de Levis is hailed by his men after the Battle of
Sainte-Foy. (Ann Ronan Picture Library)

Fraser at Quebec. (Roger-Viollet)

Chambly, stranding them on the Isle-aux-Noix. His rangers and other forces roamed the countryside, forcing Bougainville to withdraw towards St. Jean, where he met up with additional French forces and staged a further withdrawal towards Montreal. The French forces opposing de Haviland also began to suffer from desertion losses. De Haviland continued moving towards the St. Lawrence. Forward units of Murray and de Haviland made contact in early September.

Amherst encountered and fought several small French units on his march up the St. Lawrence, but nature proved the most difficult obstacle, specifically the rapids just outside Montreal. His force was somewhat battered by their crossing, but landed at La Chine, 14 km (nine miles) from Montreal, on 6 September. Montreal was slowly being surrounded.

The Marquis de Levis recognized that his force was slowly disappearing as the British advanced. Murray had crossed the St. Lawrence and began to cut off the city from the east, while Amherst set up camp to the west. De Haviland's force was approaching the city from the south. Amherst's column was beginning to move heavy artillery from La Chine. With the French forces melting away, Vaudreuil, the

French governor, and senior French military officers held a council of war to decide the next step. Negotiations with Amherst began, and on 8 September the capitulation was signed.

One aspect of the negotiated peace was that the French soldiers were to lay down their arms and promise not to serve again during the present war. Some French officers felt that this was an intolerable condition, but the number of desertions from their ranks left them powerless to negotiate. The brother of Jeffrey Amherst, William, stated the reasons for such harsh conditions on the French:

the General's [Amherst] reason which he has given for imposing such harsh terms on he regulars that they cannot return with honour is a series of bad behaviour during this present war in the country in letting ... the Indians commit the worst cruelties (William Amherst).

Some French officers considered this reason particularly hypocritical, given the British Army's own record. The British had waged a devastating war on the civilian population during 1759 in and around Quebec with not just the help of allied Indians, but brutal force imposed by their own regulars.

Thomas Brown, a Rogers' Ranger

As noted in the section dealing with the British forces, the Ranger Corps that developed in New England and Nova Scotia was considered to be an elite force, considerably feared by its French and Indian enemies. The Rangers drew most of their men from the frontier regions, selecting those considered capable of enduring the hardships of fighting in the forest. The following is an excerpt from a narrative of a ranger from the Rogers' Ranger Corps.

Thomas Brown was born in Charlestown, Massachusetts in 1740. He decided to go to war fairly early in the conflict; while serving as an apprentice, at the age of 16 he enlisted in 'Major Rogers' Corps of Rangers', joining Captain Speakman's Company in May 1756. The way the text is written implies that this was a newly raised unit. Brown describes how he and others marched to Albany, New York, where they arrived on 1 August, and then moved on to Fort Edward.

Brown's narrative relates how, upon arrival at Fort Edward, he and other Rangers were sent out on 'Scouts', which today would be defined as patrols. He mentions that, during one of these Scouts, he managed to kill an Indian. He does not, however, provide any information about the amount or type of training that he received, and the text implies that the Rangers learned their trade of scouting and ambushing on the job.

Brown's Scouts expeditions took place during the late summer, autumn and early winter months of 1756 and 1757, during the same period that French and Indian raiding parties were operating in the area. Both sides were seeking intelligence on the preparations of the forces operating around Forts William Henry and Carillon (Ticonderoga), as well as carrying out raiding parties on convoys travelling to the forts.

Although Thomas Brown does not provide details concerning his training, he does describe, in great detail, a long distance 'Scout' to ambush French and Indian supply columns operating in the Fort Carillon and Crown Point region. This Scout, which left Fort William Henry on 18 January 1757, is very likely the Battle of the Snowshoes, which is described below in more detail. According to Brown, the Scout consisted of 60 Rangers, including Major Robert Rogers, the Corps commander. All of these, according to Brown, were volunteers: 'All were Volunties that went on this Scout' (p. 5). In other words, unlike other operations, the men on this Scout chose to go rather than being ordered to do so.

Brown relates how the Rangers arrived on the road leading from Fort Carillon to Crown Point. As they came in sight of Lake Champlain, Major Rogers spotted some 50 sleighs on the lake's frozen surface. He ordered the Rangers to lay in ambush and, when the French sleighs were 'near enough ... to pursue them' (p. 5). He describes his proximity to Major Rogers as the Rangers ambushed the party, as well as the Rangers' capture of seven Frenchmen in the raid. (He also notes that many men from the sleighs managed to escape, either to Crown Point or Fort Carillon, alerting the French and Indians based at both forts to the presence of Rogers and his Scout.) The Rangers interrogated the prisoners and learned that there were 500 French Regulars based at Fort Carillon. Major Rogers decided that the Scout should return to Fort William Henry and that, due to the amount of snow on the ground, they would return the same way they had come, outfitted with snowshoes. The French and Indians in the area, alerted to the Rangers' presence, set out to destroy Rogers and his men.

Within a few hours of the march, the Scout was spotted and attacked. Brown describes how:

We march'd in an Indian-File and kept the Prisoners in the Rear, lest we should be attack'd: We proceeded in this Order about a Mile and a half, and as we were ascending a Hill, and the Centre of our Men were at the Top, the French, to the number of 400, besides 30 or 40 Indians, fir'd on us before we discovered them (p. 6).

Major Rogers ordered his Rangers to advance, sending them into withering fire. Brown describes what happened to him and some of the other men, highlighting the brutal reality of eighteenth century forest warfare. He states that:

I receiv'd a Wound from the Enemy ... thro' the Body, upon which I retir'd into the Rear, to the Prisoner I had taken on the Lake, knock'd him on the Head and killed him, lest he should Escape and give Information to the Enemy (p. 6).

Brown was almost killed by two Indians as he withdrew to the rear of the column. However, he was able to form himself, with other Rangers, into a small box of men. The fighting in the area was intense, as Brown describes:

[I] got to the Centre of our Men, and fix'd myself behind a large Pine, where I loaded and fir'd every Opportunity; after I had discharged 6 or 7 Times, there came a Ball and cut off my Gun just at the Lock. About half an Hour after, I receiv'd a Shot in my Knee; I crawled again into the Rear, and as I was turning about receiv'd a Shot in my Shoulder (p. 6).

Brown speculates that the fighting lasted for five and half hours, and notes that, while they were surrounded, the Rangers were not overwhelmed during the daylight hours. Brown contends that the Rangers inflicted more than 60 casualties on the French and Indian troops, and describes what happened as night drew in:

The Engagement held, as near as I could guess, 5 and half Hours... By the Time it grew dark and the Firing Ceased on both Sides, and as we were so few the Major [Rogers] took the Advantage of the Night and escaped with all the well Men, without informing the wounded of his Design, lest they should inform the Enemy and they should pursue him before he had got out of their Reach (p. 6).

Brown was able to make it to Captain Speakman; they and another badly wounded Ranger, named Baker, were able to make a small fire. They could not hear or see any other Rangers in the vicinity; at one moment, Captain Speakman called out to Major Rogers but received no answer. The wounded men were unable to travel, and hope of escape began to dwindle as they heard the enemy approaching. The men decided to surrender to the French, at which point Brown appears to have slipped away from the other two men at the fire. Brown's account of what occurred next says:

I crawl'd so far from the Fire that I could not be seen, though I could see what was acted at the Fire; the Indian came to Capt. Spikeman [Speakman], who was not able to resist, and stripp'd and scalp'd him alive; Baker, who was lying by the Captain, pull'd out his Knife to stab himself, which the Indian prevented and carried him away (p. 7).

Speakman, who was still alive after this attack, pleaded with Brown to kill him. Brown refused, and moved off in order to avoid a similar fate. Since he had no shoes, and the snow was quite deep, he found progress difficult. (Speakman was later beheaded by the Indians). He attempted to move around various French sentry positions and at one point, came close to being seen by a French soldier. Brown survived the night in an agony of discomfort, without adequate clothing or shoes. Around 11am the next morning, he was spotted by a small group of Indians. They rushed him and he thought it would be best to be killed outright instead of being scalped alive. He describes how:

I threw off my Blanket, and Fear and Dread quickened my Pace for a while; but, by Reason of the Loss of so much Blood from my Wounds, I soon fail'd. When they were within a few Rods of me they cock'd their Guns, and told me to stop; but I refus'd, hoping they would fire and Kill me on the spot; which I chose, rather then the dreadful Death Capt. Spikeman [sic] died of. They soon came up with me, took me by the Neck and Kiss'd me. ... They took some dry Leaves and put them into my Wounds, and then turn'd about and ordered me to follow them (p. 8).

Thomas Brown served out the remainder of the war as a captive, both of French military officers and various Indians. He travelled as far as the Mississippi River, to the west, and the Montreal region, to the north. He was returned to the British forces on 25 November 1759, after more than two years of captivity, and returned to Charlestown at the beginning of January 1760.

The economic and civilian costs

In pure economic terms, the war in both North America and the rest of the world cost France and Great Britain considerably. Britain had to pay for the upkeep of major armies in North America and Germany. The expense of building naval vessels was also significant. Even with tax levies throughout the war, the debt rose annually, and the British government was forced to borrow to make good on the shortfall. Britain did have one economic bonus during this period: the Royal Navy was dominant on the seas by 1759 and thus was able both to seize war booty and to deny access to French ports. In 1756, Great Britain's national debt was 75 million pounds; by the end of the conflict it had climbed to 133 million pounds. The continuing need to maintain garrison troops after 1763 were the principal reasons for the controversial demand that the wealthy Thirteen Colonies to take on some of the costs of their own protection in the 1760s.

France was in much the same financial position as Great Britain. However, France decided to borrow more money rather than levy taxes on the population. Unlike Britain, her trade suffered heavily from the Royal Navy blockade of the French ports, causing a further loss of revenue during the conflict. In 1753 the national debt was 1,360 million livres. By the end of the conflict the national debt had nearly doubled, climbing to 2,350 million livres. It cost 24.5 million livres a year just to keep the French armies in the field; most of this was spent on the regular army in Germany.

The war also proved a major financial drain on the Thirteen Colonies and New France. Each of the Thirteen Colonies provided varying levels of support in the form of supplies, provincial troops, recruits for regular regiments, and billeting of troops. Some colonies, such as South Carolina, were not particularly willing to support the war effort; this was often linked to the level of belief in the cause of the war demonstrated by elected and appointed officials. As the fortunes of war began to turn in Britain's favor, some colonies grew less enthusiastic about committing money and men to a campaign happening far away to the north of them. Others saw the threat diminish in their own region and decided that the war was not as important as they had previously believed.

The British commander-in-chief periodically had to rely upon local merchants for specie, or borrow money to pay for supplies and provisions for the coming year. Shipments of money from Great Britain often arrived later than officers would have preferred. In 1759, General Amherst called upon the New York Assembly for a loan to pay for his campaign. In both New France and the Thirteen Colonies, many merchants and business people came to rely upon government and military clients for the main part of their business. One issue that did not affect the Thirteen Colonies was shortage of food, for either civilians or soldiers. While the soldiers may have been restricted at times during the campaigns, the civilian population did not have rationing imposed upon them, unlike New France.

The colonies were asked each year to provide provincial soldiers for campaign duty. This entailed men serving outside their respective colonies. Each year a new force was raised, and then released from duty at the end of the campaign season. The British government provided subsidies for the raising of these forces. Regardless, by 1759 assemblymen from several colonies asserted that the colonies could no longer provide the numbers needed. Considerable numbers of provincial troops had been lost to battle or sickness; other men seeking adventure or pay had also left the colonies to enlist in the Royal Navy or the British regulars. Colonial leaders feared that the constant drain would have a negative effect on colonial farming and trades. They were also angered by the British government's method of handling the issue: each year the British government provided subsidies for the past campaign season, reimbursing the Thirteen Colonies for about 40 percent of their total military expenses. As the new campaign season approached, officials would threaten not to pay the subsidies owed unless each colony provided the desired number of soldiers.

The numbers of soldiers provided and the money raised by each colony also became a sore point between the colonies. Colonies such as Massachusetts Bay, Connecticut, New York, New Jersey, New Hampshire, and Rhode Island provided considerable support to the war effort. They were resentful of the smaller amounts of support provided by other colonies such as Georgia, South and North Carolina, and Maryland. Georgia was a poor colony and was unable to raise provincial troops; the colony's security was provided for by British regulars. South Carolina only provided for three companies of provincial infantry and two of horse. North Carolina and Maryland were criticized for not providing any major support to the war effort; both of these colonies felt less threatened by the conflict than their neighbors to the north. The border colonies of Pennsylvania and Virginia provided sufficient men and support for the war effort as long as they felt directly threatened, but as the war in the west dwindled and the focus shifted to the invasion of Canada, their support began to dry up as well.

This constant need for soldiers and supplies from the colonies was an ongoing source of friction between British military officials and colonial assemblymen. Each side accused the other of not carrying its share of the load or of being autocratic. The debate became so acrimonious that even the end of the war did not resolve it and argument, continued through the financial crises of the postwar period. It eventually led

to more drastic demands by the British government and, eventually, war between Britain and the Thirteen Colonies.

The situation in New France was overall more difficult. One of the major problems was the food supply, which proved to be insufficient on more than one occasion. One possible reason for this was the fact that only a small portion of the province had been cultivated properly. This level of cultivation was satisfactory during the peace years, but when war broke out demand increased. The crop yield, which had been sufficient for the population as well as supplies to the Marines, militia, and allied Indians, could not stretch to accommodate the 6,000 regular soldiers who were shipped to New France during the war. The plan was that soldiers would be shipped with their own provisions, and that each year a large supply convoy would arrive from France to support the offensive operations of the campaign season.

The reality, however, was that due to the successful Royal Navy blockade, the number of ships that arrived each year dwindled steadily. The situation reached crisis point in 1757. A large flotilla arrived with stores, but it was still not enough to support both the soldiers and citizens of New France. Montcalm recorded that 'provisions fail the people, reduced to a quarter pound of bread. Perhaps the rations of the soldiers must be reduced again' (Sautai, pp. 38–39). In June 1757, all grain was centrally stored and made into bread by the colonial government. Daily allowances were allocated to all the people within the colony. Nature also had a role to play in the colony's plight; the harvests for 1756 and 1757 were poor, followed by the unusually severe winter of 1757–58. The population was forced to consume the seed crop of wheat for the following year. France responded and three ships were sent with seed, which reached their destination.

The results of the harvest had an additional effect on the army: the composition of the colonial militia. The militia, as described previously, was drawn from all sectors of the French community, including farmers. If the threat to New France did not subside for a significant period of time and the men could not be released, the yield of the harvest might be adversely affected. As a result, at times militiamen took matters into their own hands and returned to their farms without having been discharged. Widespread desertion, in turn, put French commanders in a precarious position. The two conflicting priorities created an apparently insoluble dilemma.

Corruption was another major issue for New France. The colony's chief colonial administrator, Francois Bigot, had created a monopoly on goods sold within the colony to benefit himself and some of his friends. With the advent of war, the principal products sold in New France were no longer furs, fish, or skins, but military provisions and supplies. Bigot was in charge of the contracts for military stores supplied to the troops, and he and his cronies were lining their pockets. When food was rationed, the sale of bread also came under Bigot's control, when the French Crown bought the grain and made it into bread. The prices that the Crown paid for the flour were set and controlled by Bigot, as was the price of bread sold to colonists.

Paper currency in New France was steadily devalued over the course of the war. French attempts to send specie to the colony only sped up the process. Farmers only sold to soldiers who had been paid in specie, and both civilians and soldiers hoarded the coins. New France was paying over 12 million livres a year by 1757 for the upkeep of New France. By 1758, the British blockade and the shift within the French court to a Continental strategy had left New France almost abandoned. Ships with food, supplies, soldiers, or currency were diverted to other regions, and New France was left to defend itself.

Portions of the civilian populations of both sides suffered directly as a result of the war, and there were examples of outright 'cruelty' by both sides. One of the most famous cases is the expulsion of the Acadian (French) population from Nova Scotia by the British. After the capture of Fort Beausejour in 1755, the question arose of what to do

with the Acadians. Many colonial governors, such as William Shirley of Massachusetts, considered them a nuisance and a risk to the security of Nova Scotia. The situation came to a head when the British produced an oath of allegiance to the British Crown, and required Acadians to adhere to it. Many of the Acadians, however, preferred to remain neutral. They had no desire to swear allegiance and wished to be exempt from military duty. British commanders reported that their mood changed from neutral to hostile when rumors began to circulate of a French fleet arriving in the Bay of Fundy.

The British were in a difficult position. The Acadians lived on a particularly strategic piece of land, and the war had just begun in earnest. There were also British land speculators waiting to cash on the excellent lands occupied by the Acadian farms.

British military and colonial officials met in Halifax, and determined that the Acadians should be forcibly removed from their homes and transported to the Thirteen Colonies. They decided against sending them to Quebec or Louisbourg because in either place they would provide valuable reinforcements for the militia. The Acadian villages were emptied and the settlers marshaled towards the Bay of Fundy where, over the course of autumn 1755, ships arrived from the Thirteen Colonies to transport the people. The British authorities did their best to keep villages and families together, so as not to cause further psychological damage to the uprooted Acadians.

In the end more than 6,000 men, women and children were transported. Some Acadians, upon receiving word of the British plan, escaped to Quebec. Other groups of people withdrew into the woods of Nova Scotia. Some of the men in these groups carried out a guerrilla campaign over the coming years. Many of the Acadian homes and farms were burned to prevent escaped refugees returning to their homes. The British government also hoped that people would surrender to British authorities after they realized their position was hopeless. Many of the Acadians who were sent to the

Exile of the Acadians. (National Archives of Canada)

Thirteen Colonies eventually made their way to Louisiana. Some returned to Acadia after the Treaty of Paris and continue to live in the same districts today. The story of the Acadians was later made famous in Longfellow's poem 'Evangeline'.

The British continued this policy for most of the war. Following the seizure of Louisbourg in 1758, General Amherst decided to round up and transport the civilian populations in and around Louisbourg, as well as the French colonists on St. Jean Island (Prince Edward Island). All colonists who took up arms were considered prisoners of war and were subsequently transported to Great Britain along with the French soldiers. Colonists who did not take up arms were transported to France. More than 8,000 people were transported from Cape Breton and St. Jean Island. Amherst decided on this policy after the killings at Fort William Henry. He felt that the French deserved such treatment after what he considered their leniency in allowing the Indians to commit such crimes against civilians.

Warfare all along the frontier was brutal. Many white settlers on both sides were taken prisoner or killed by roaming bands of allied Indians, French militia, and rangers. This type of random violence had occurred for many years since the mid-1600s, but the onset of the French-Indian War provided a new impetus to spread fear along the frontier. The British forces, especially the rangers, were able to launch waterborne attacks into the heartland of New France and against Indian settlements along the St. Lawrence. Major General Amherst cited the abuses of the French and their Indian allies when he drew up the conditions of surrender at Montreal in 1760.

French regular soldiers generally did not come into immediate contact with the civilian population of the Thirteen Colonies. Some were involved in small-scale raids along the frontier or in clearing lands of British settlers. The major British towns did not have to contend with foreign occupation. The civilian population of New France, on the other hand, had to accommodate the presence not only of British-allied Indians and rangers, but from

1758–60 had to contend with British Army regular soldiers as well.

The major evidence of French civilians suffering at the hands of British regulars occurred during the Quebec Campaign in 1759. Major General Wolfe apparently issued orders for the destruction of the countryside. His reasoning for this was twofold: first, to deny supplies to the French garrison on the north bank of the St. Lawrence River; and second, to attempt to force Montcalm to battle. Two journal entries by British soldiers give insight into the actions of some of the British regulars at Quebec. A Sergeant-Major from a grenadier company described the actions outside Quebec:

on the 20th [August] the Louisbourg Grenadiers began their march down the main land of Quebec, in order to burn and destroy all the houses on that side … [On] the 25th began to destroy the country, burning houses, cutting down corn and the like (Sergeant-Major, p. 16).

An officer with the 15th Foot also described his experiences on a march through the countryside outside Quebec. His action, like the Sergeant-Major's, took place in August 1759. He recalled:

our light infantry and rangers marched off to the Parish of St. Nicola but a little after we passed the church of St. Antonia our advanced guard was fired upon by a party of the enemy that lay in ambush in the wood … [W]e marched to the far end of the parish when we began to burn all before us (Add Mss 45662).

The British were not always given orders to ravage the countryside; in fact it appears that sometimes the opposite happened. During the 1760 campaign, some units were ordered not to abuse the population as they marched towards Montreal. A Massachusetts provincial soldier named Sergeant David Holden noted that, when his regiment marched from Chambly to Montreal, the French population was generally very civil. He commented that

the French treat us on our march with the utmost civility more over our army was very cautious in not abusing any of them or their subsistance … General Amherst returns the troops under his command abundance of thanks for their so strickly observing his orders (Holden, p. 21).

The severity of the fighting along the frontier during the early years of the conflict created ugly situations. The attacks by the French and their allied Indians spread fear and hatred among the colonists. The killing of British civilians after the surrender of Fort William Henry provided the impetus for British reprisals when troops entered civilian areas of New France.

Jean Lowry and Titus King

Capture of colonists by Indian troops was a common feature of the French-Indian War. Two contemporary accounts of English citizens who were captives of the French-allied Indians describe very different types of treatment. One of the accounts was written by a woman and the other by a man. The first described here is a harrowing account by a woman who was seized, along with her children.

Jean Lowry was living on the frontier region of Pennsylvania when, in April 1755, a band of Indians arrived outside her homestead. They immediately killed her husband, and then, as she states: '[there] being no man in the house at that time the barbarians rushed into the house, plundered the house and did what they pleased … [T]hey set fire to the house' (1 April 1755). Mrs Lowry and her five children were seized and forced to march overland.

After traveling for four days, a group of 50 white settlers caught up with the Indian party and fired upon them. The white settlers were able to release Mrs Lowry and her children, but their ordeal was not yet over. That evening, a larger Indian party returned and attacked the camp of the white settlers. Mrs Lowry recalled that

the savages returned and surrounded our people this gave them great advantage … [O]ur people did the best they could for two hours. A great many of our people were killed and wounded … [O]ne wounded man was tortured and the ladies had to watch (5 April 1755).

The whites from the party who were left alive and could still march were taken as prisoners.

Mrs Lowry and her family were ordered to march on after the man being tortured had finally died. When the Indian party reached a hunting camp, Mrs Lowry began a period of intense hardship. She described the Indians

laying upon me with their [hot] rods I being so weak and spent with fatigue could not run … so they had their leisure to exercise their barbarous customs upon my feeble body, this left many wounds on me (8 April 1755).

It was also at this point that her eight-year-old son was taken away from her.

The Indian party marched the white prisoners into an Indian village a few days later. As they entered both Mrs Lowry and her eldest daughter were given 'an awful beating' (10 April 1755). Many of the other white prisoners were 'adopted' by Indian households, and here Mrs Lowry lost her eldest daughter who was 10, and another daughter who was six, to Indian families. As she continued marching up the Allegheny River with the two children still with her, she came across the son that she had lost, but was not allowed to collect him. Mrs Lowry was a religious person, and believed that her condition and losses over the past weeks must be 'for our sins that god has delivered us into the hands of the Indians' (17 April 1755).

It appears that one important reason for the treatment that Mrs Lowry particularly received was her resolve not to be seen to cooperate with the Indians in any way – either by accepting adoption by Indians or by doing any work for them. On 23 April, the Indian party entered another village, where Mrs Lowry was beaten by several Indian women for the loss of their husbands. In this village, her two remaining children were also taken from her, although one was returned to her later in the day (24 April 1755).

Image of a captured white woman and her Indian captors. (Amon Carter Museum, Fort Worth)

At this point, Mrs Lowry admitted that she began to moderate her behavior and to try to accept her predicament. One reason for this change of heart was that 'the Indians had threatened to sell me to the French and what cruel usage I would meet with from them' (5 May 1755). She left the Indian village for Fort Venango under the ownership of another Indian warrior. While in Fort Venango, she gave birth to another little girl, who died the same day (4 July 1755). This event makes clear that Mrs Lowry was in fact pregnant throughout the time she was marching overland. The beatings and generally poor treatment she received must have played a role in the death of the child.

The journal's pace quickens after Mrs Lowry arrived at Fort Venango, where she remained as a servant of the French commanding officer from 15 May 1755 until 27 July 1757. The French commander's wife took Mrs Lowry when she traveled from Fort Venango to Fort Niagara, and then to Montreal. In Montreal, she heard that white prisoners were being exchanged for French prisoners, and she continued to serve as a servant in Montreal until she received word of a possible exchange. In September 1758, she was allowed to proceed to Quebec City, where she was exchanged for French captives. On 16 March 1759, she returned to New York after being shipped to Great Britain. The journal records no mention of seeing any of her children ever again.

It is interesting to note how the journal of a male captive named Titus King differs from Mrs Lowry; he appears to have avoided most of the brutality that she suffered. King was a provincial soldier in Colonel Israel Williams' Regiment, Massachusetts. He and a small party of soldiers were stationed at Charlemont, 40 km (25 miles) northwest of Northampton, Massachusetts, to protect the local farming community from Indian and French irregulars. On 11 June 1755 his small band of men was attacked by a larger group of Indian warriors, and King was captured along with a small boy soldier. He noted that 'we marched 20 or 25 miles on the first day'. It is interesting to note that King's Indian captors seemed to value their prisoners rather highly. He commented that when 'the boy was not able to go any more the Indians carried him on their backs and put me to carry a pack and a gun' (12 June 1755).

The food for the trip was meager for the prisoners, and King commented on 17 June that

since we have had nothing to eat except a pigeon and an owl they killed on the way roots green barks of the tree and the like ... we was very faint and hungry ... [T]he Indians filled a large littal of this pounded corn and boiled it ... eat very heartily but I could not eat so much as I thought I should (17 June 1755).

The Indian party was marching towards Crown Point.

King and his Indian captors reached their destination in early July. King commented on the good behavior of the French officers and men: 'the French treated me pretty well with the wine and brandy and good manners'. The next day, 18 July, King left with his Indian captors, traveling by canoe up Lake Champlain towards St. Jean. One evening the Indians got very drunk and the next day, due to their hangovers, King was forced to be one of the oarsmen on one of the canoes for some of the day. It was while the Indian party was traveling on Lake Champlain that King was told that he was not going to Montreal to be exchanged, but was to become an Indian and go with the warriors to their village. One of the warriors commented, 'Frenchmen no good, Englishmen no good, Indian very good' (21 July 1755).

It appears that King accepted his new role. He was stripped of his shirt and had his hair cut and his face painted. The party arrived at St. Jean on 22 July, where once again King was treated well. He noted, perhaps a bit regretfully, that 'the French treated me pretty well ... [but] I must live with them [Indians] in their wigwams' instead of accepting the French offer to stay with them (22 July 1755). King, repainted, and the Indians moved out on 23 July for the Indian village. On 25 July they arrived at the Indian village, where they were greeted by 200 Indians on the shore of the river. King described how the 'young Indians had sticks to whip us' (25 June 1755). He was ordered to run about 30 rods up a hill, with a crowd on both sides. He expected to be beaten, but the crowd dispersed as he ran up the hill and he was not. He had apparently been accepted as part of the village.

As he noted, however, he was still a captive of one of the Indian warriors. He remained part of the village for the rest of 1755, all of 1756, and most of 1757. As many Indian warriors left the village to fight, King became an important male figure. He was adopted as a grandfather by one of the families after their grandfather failed to return. It was expected that King would have an Indian woman and have children to help populate the village. He was formally put in Indian dress and accepted as an Indian. During the campaign season of 1757, he left with a band of warriors for Fort William Henry. However, he was sold to the French for 120 livres and sent to Montreal. He was then exchanged by the French, and by the summer of 1758, he had returned to Northampton via Great Britain.

Titus King had not endured the incredible suffering that Mrs. Lowry had lived through. This may have been partly due to the value the Indians placed on a male captive over a female captive. It may also have been due to the fact that King seemed resigned to his fate and did what he was told, whereas Mrs. Lowry had put up considerable resistance.

Treaty of Paris and the Indian uprising

The capture of Montreal more or less brought the war in North America to an end, but the larger conflict, the Seven Years' War, dragged on outside North America for another two years. Prussia, in alliance with Great Britain, continued a defensive war against Russia and Austria, and war with France continued on the continent as well. The British also provided ongoing funding and men to His Britannic Majesty's Army campaign against the French in Hanover. France and Great Britain also continued to wage war in the colonies of the Caribbean and India. Spain entered the conflict on France's side in 1761. The British had become very proficient in amphibious operations by 1760, and the Royal Navy was dominant on the seas. Campaigns against the Spanish and French colonies in the Caribbean, India, and the Philippines were all great successes for Britain. The war finally came to an end more as a product of exhaustion on the part of all parties involved than any definitive victory. For more detail, see Essential Histories *The Seven Years' War*.

Two peace treaties formally concluded the Seven Years' War. The first, signed by France, Great Britain, and Spain, was agreed on 10 February 1763 and known as the Treaty of Paris. The second, known as the Treaty of Hubertusburg, was concluded between Austria and Prussia on 15 February 1763. Only the Treaty of Paris will be examined here, since it had ramifications for the conflict in North America.

Great Britain's portion of the treaty has been characterized as swapping snow for sugar cane and sun. All of the French lands east of the Mississippi River were awarded to Britain, including the Ohio River valley, which had been one of the principal causes of the conflict. Quebec and Cape Breton were also ceded to Great Britain. Of all her North American possessions, France was allowed to retain control of only two small islands off the coast of Newfoundland, St. Pierre and Miquelon. In exchange, France received the islands of Guadeloupe and Martinique, which she had lost during the conflict. Britain also took possession of Florida from Spain, in exchange for the Philippines and Cuba. Great Britain was now the only major European power on the Atlantic Seaboard of North America, controlling the entire coastline from Newfoundland in the north to Florida in the south.

Even with Great Britain in undisputed control of the area, problems arose almost immediately in the newly acquired territories of the Ohio River valley and the lands west of the Appalachians. The French had maintained forts and a small settler presence in the region, but had infringed little upon the local Indian population. With the British in control, some of the British colonists wished to push west from the Atlantic seaboard and open up the interior for settlement. Naturally, the Indians who were already living in the area objected to this plan, and the determination of the white settlers to carry on regardless led to a large-scale Indian uprising, known as Pontiac's Rebellion, in 1763–64.

When fighting ended in 1760 after the seizure of Montreal, Rogers' Rangers and the 60th Regiment were sent to occupy the French forts in the west, at Detroit and along the Great Lakes. The troops were given orders to accept the surrender of the French forces in the region, meet with various Indian chiefs, and explain that Great Britain had taken control of the area. Soldiers and officers were also instructed not to give the Indians gifts, ammunition, or guns, a policy which offended the Indians in the region who had recently been waging war against the British and expected to be rewarded for promising loyalty to the new government. The soldiers were warned not to give offense to any one group; peace was to be maintained at all costs.

Not only did the British disappoint the Indians who had been allied with the French; they also alienated the Senecas, one of the tribes of the Six Nations, who considered that the British had failed to keep promises made during the war. To persuade Indian tribes to side with them, the British had signed agreements promising that lands west of the Alleghenies would only be used by Indians for hunting. Trading of European goods in these areas would be cheaper and fur and skins would sell at higher prices.

As early as 1761, Indian representatives, including members of the Six Nations, demanded a meeting with the governor of Pennsylvania. The Indians contended that the British were not keeping to their promises. White settlers were moving into the region west of the Alleghenies, goods were still being sold at high prices, and furs and skins were not appreciating in value. The Indian representatives also stated a further concern, that 'there are forts all round us and therefore we are apprehensive that death is coming upon us' (Bouquet, Mss 21655). Indians who had sided with the British were also not allowed to move west into territory formerly belonging to the French. This proscription irked many Indians, who felt they had scores to settle with the French-allied tribes, and who wanted access to the hunting grounds in the Ohio River valley.

The white settlers, for their part, felt they had a perfect right to settle where they chose. Captain Bouquet of the 60th soon became an unpopular figure, since he did what he could to arrest whites operating illegally in the region. To make matters worse, a set of orders was then handed down that Indians could be given small gifts for capturing illegal white settlers and bringing them to outposts of the 60th along the frontier (Bouquet, MSS21653). White settlers found in the area had to demonstrate their purpose for being there and

present proper paperwork. Failing to do so meant that they would be arrested, and under the circumstances they were subject to military, not civilian law. White settlers were furious at what they perceived as the army's favoring the Indians over them, and the soldiers' performance of their duty progressively soured relations between settlers and regulars.

Given the size of the area that the soldiers had to patrol, white settlers were able to elude them without great difficulty, slip into the prohibited areas, and carry out large-scale hunting west of the Appalachians. The Indians in the region grew increasingly restless about these incursions, and clashes between Indians and settlers began to occur. By 1761, the Senecas, a formerly British-allied tribe, were holding meetings with members of the Delawares and Miamis to discuss attacks on the frontier region forts. They did agree that they were not ready for an all-out rebellion. At the same time as the war raged in Europe and the rest of the world, French settlers in the area began to fan the flames by meeting with various Indian chiefs and discussing a possible return of the French to the region.

By 1762, the British troops on the frontier were in a difficult position, caught between white settlers and Indian tribes. Bouquet recognized the potential for even greater trouble and attempted to reinforce the various forts, preparing them for a possible outbreak of violence. Bouquet also advised General Amherst, commander-in-chief North America, of the rising tension on the frontier and asked for further reinforcements. Most of the troops from North America were involved in the amphibious campaign in the Caribbean, however, so sufficient reinforcement was not possible.

The Indian uprising began in late 1762 when Seneca warriors killed two white settlers. War belts were sent by the Senecas to the western tribes as the signal to begin hostilities. While extremely dangerous to those in the frontier region, the uprising was not a completely unanimous effort. Members of the Senecas, Ottawas, Hurons, Delawares, and Miamis participated, but no tribe involved all of its warriors. Additionally, none of the western tribes, such as the Sauks, Puans, and Foxes, raised the war belt.

The purpose of the Indian uprising is still unclear. Its principal objective seems to have been the seizure of all British forts and posts, but then even this strategy was not implemented with any consistency. Particularly at first, the Indian effort was not a coordinated onslaught, but seemingly unrelated attacks on various forts by groups of warriors.

One indication of the fact that the Indian uprising was not as widespread or organized as it could have been was the conduct of one Indian chief, Pontiac. He was an Ottawa chief who only commanded a local village near Fort Detroit. He agreed with other Indian chiefs about the state of affairs under British governance, but instead of acting in conjunction with others, he set up a campaign against Fort Detroit by himself. Pontiac did not participate in any other actions, but Fort Detroit was such an important outpost that the British hailed him as the leading war chief and the entire uprising became known as Pontiac's Rebellion.

In early April 1763, Pontiac gathered various Indian warriors near Fort Detroit and called for action against the British fort. On 1 May Pontiac himself arrived at Fort Detroit with a small reconnaissance party to assess the British defenses and troops. He was greeted and entertained by the British commander, Major Gladwin, after which the Indian party left, promising to return at a later date. The British, although they were aware of the possibility of attack, still did not want to aggravate the situation by not being amicable. Pontiac met with another party of Indian warriors on 5 May and called for the extermination of the British at Fort Detroit. Other Indian warriors decided to join as word reached Pontiac that other forts were also going to be attacked. On 7 May, a select group of warriors marched towards Fort Detroit with weapons hidden and a plan to storm the fort.

Gladwin had received information that an attack was imminent, and had 100 men under his command. He decided to close the gates and put white traders in the area under arms to boost defensive numbers. Pontiac acted surprised when he came upon the Fort and was not received with open gates. On 8 May, other chiefs attempted to meet with Gladwin to promise that the Indians had no intention of seizing the fort. Gladwin dismissed these claims and prepared for an armed encounter. On 9 May, an armed flotilla of Indian canoes arrived. Gladwin continued to refuse to speak with the Indians, and on 10 May the siege of Fort Detroit formally began. A relief force of 95 soldiers marching toward the fort was surrounded and overwhelmed on 29 May.

Other forts along the Great Lakes and in the Ohio River valley were subsequently attacked by other Indian tribes. Some forts were seized by a surprise attack; others were able to repel the Indian attacks and then the garrison slip away during the evening. The Seneca attack at Fort Venango destroyed relations between the British and their former allies; a Seneca war party was received into the fort as allies, only to turn and massacre the garrison. By the end of June, all of the British forts along the frontier and in the newly claimed territories had been seized except for Forts Pitt, Detroit, and Niagara. Indian war parties also headed east toward Fort Bedford but were unsuccessful in capturing it. Fort Pitt was surrounded in late June, but not attacked until late July. The British managed to repulse the Indian attack, when it came, knowing that it was critical to hold Fort Pitt, as well as Niagara and Detroit, as jumping-off positions for the re-conquest of the Ohio River valley and Great Lakes Region. Colonel Bouquet and his headquarters received word of the attacks by late May.

On 28 July a relief column arrived at Fort Detroit. This force numbered 200 men drawn from regular and ranger units, but was carrying few supplies or provisions for the fort. On 31 July, the column, commanded by Captain James Dalyell, marched to destroy the Indian camp and lift the siege. They were ambushed and all but destroyed at a creek named Bloody Run, with more than 20 men killed, 30 wounded, and 100 captured. Captain Dalyell was killed in the battle, and the siege of Detroit continued.

All available troops were sent to Philadelphia to stage an expedition to relieve Fort Pitt. At this point, not only had several regiments been transported to the Caribbean to fight in the campaigns there, but the war in North America had also officially ended and many more men had been shipped home or discharged from service. Bouquet gathered a force of men from the 42nd, 77th, and 60th Regiments of Foot, as well as rangers, to open the road to Fort Pitt. He had only about 500 men with him.

Bouquet's force marched overland to Carlisle and moved out toward Fort Pitt on 18 July. They had been delayed, as previously, while the local colonial governments took their time gathering supplies for the force. The Indians besieging

Fort Pitt received word of Bouquet's movement and moved east to ambush his force. The two groups met at a place named Bushy Run, 40 km (25 miles) from Fort Pitt. On the morning of 5 August, Bouquet's forward units skirmished with Indian warriors. Bouquet, realizing that his force was in a potential ambush situation, deployed his troops in a circular defensive position and awaited the Indian attack. It came at 1.00 pm and lasted throughout the afternoon and into the evening. Bouquet's circle held out, despite many casualties. On the morning of 6 August, the Indians attacked again, undertaking coordinated attacks immediately. When Bouquet recognized that he was in danger of being breached, he decided to shorten his lines, and two light companies were ordered to fall back. The Indians saw this, mistook it for a retreat, and launched a disorganized attack.

Battle of Bushy Run, 1763

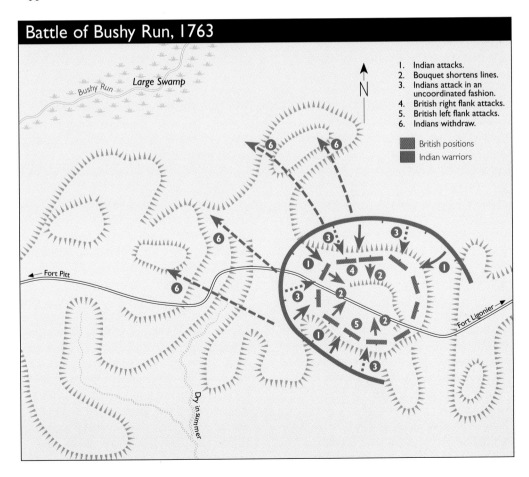

1. Indian attacks.
2. Bouquet shortens lines.
3. Indians attack in an uncoordinated fashion.
4. British right flank attacks.
5. British left flank attacks.
6. Indians withdraw.

British positions
Indian warriors

Large Swamp

Bushy Run

Fort Pitt

Fort Ligonier

Dry in Summer

Unbeknownst to the Indians, the British had already pulled back four other companies, and the right flank of the British circle began to pour heavy fire into the attacking Indian mass, then rushed them with bayonets. The British left flank attacked the Indian mass next; the Indians attempted to withdraw, but were cut down. Bouquet related that 'two other companies were so posted as to catch them [Indians] in their retreat and entirely dispersed them, and the whole fled' (Jeffrey Amherst, p. 318). The remainder of the Indian force managed to withdraw from the field of battle. It is debatable whether Bouquet calculated the whole maneuver; what is certain, however, is that he wished to shorten his lines, recognized the tactical advantage given to him, and pushed home his attack. The battle cost both sides some 50 killed and 50 wounded.

Fort Pitt was relieved by 10 August, after which Bouquet decided that his force needed rest and decided to postpone further advances into the Ohio River valley. Small detachments were sent out to Forts Bedford and Ligionier, and provincial troops arrived at Fort Pitt in early September. Bouquet then marched towards Fort Detroit while a second column of regulars retook Presque Isle. Colonel Johnson had been meeting with members of the Six Nations concerning the Senecas who had turned on the British. The Six Nations were still officially on the side of the British throughout the crisis, and vowed to deal with the traitors. Meanwhile, the Senecas kept fighting, ambushing a relief column heading out from Fort Niagara to Fort Detroit. Another column of 90 British regulars sent out to attack the Indians was also ambushed and destroyed by the Senecas. The garrisons at Fort Pitt and Detroit readied themselves for the coming winter. Fort Detroit's siege had been lifted on 15 October, but this had happened largely because the Indians had lost interest in continuing the siege. Detroit was still in dire need of supplies.

The tension in the region which provoked the Indian uprising eventually forced the British government to proclam a policy concerning the newly conquered territories. The Royal Proclamation of 1763 was an attempt to resolve several outstanding issues in the region conclusively, but it was still somewhat ambiguous. The principal conditions of the proclamation were: that the French settlements north of New York and New England were to become known as the new colony of Quebec; that Florida was to be divided into two new colonies, East and West Florida; that all three new colonies were to operate under English law; and that all other land not encompassed by the three new colonies was to belong to the Indians. Colonial governments that claimed land in the region, such as Pennsylvania and Virginia, were no longer allowed to grant lands in the area. Only Crown representatives could negotiate with Indians over the sale of land. No whites were to settle the region, and any whites already present in the region were ordered to withdraw to east of the Appalachian mountains. White traders were allowed to cross into Indian territory, but were required to carry a license from the commander-in-chief. The proclamation was vague about what French inhabitants of the Indian territory should do. Were they required to move to Quebec? The document was unclear on this issue.

The proclamation succeeded in achieving its objective, which was to end the Indian uprising. At the same time, it established a whole new set of problems with colonists from the Thirteen Colonies who wished to settle in the region, which would contribute to tension already developing.

General Amherst was replaced on 17 November 1763 by Major General Thomas Gage. Amherst had developed the strategy for 1764 before he left; provincials and regulars would be raised in New York to lift the siege of Fort Niagara, and under the command of Colonel Bradstreet, would be sent to subdue the Indians on the Great Lakes. Bouquet and his troops would march into the Ohio River valley and subdue the Indian tribes there. Colonel Johnson, assuming these campaigns were successful, would negotiate a treaty with the Indians and settle the uprising. Intelligence reports indicated that the Indians were growing tired of the situation. The siege of Detroit, in particular, had carried on longer than they had expected, and the British success at the battle of Bushy Run had broken the Indians' resolve. Johnson and Bradstreet arrived at Fort Niagara in early July to meet with a number of tribal chiefs who wished to discuss peace terms. Johnson managed to reach agreement with all but three of them. The terms of the treaty were not as harsh as might have been expected under the circumstances; the Indians were given several concessions, including the right to lodge complaints at Fort Detroit and a schedule for setting values on goods and skins.

Following the peace conference, Bradstreet left with his force to subdue the three tribes still in rebellion, and to spread the word that hostilities with the other tribes were at an end. Bouquet, as planned, moved into the Ohio River valley to subdue any remaining Indian hostility and receive any white captives. The campaign was over by the end of the year, and the frontier was peaceful once again.

Ramifications for the future

Since the French-Indian War was fought chiefly between France and Great Britain and their Indian allies, the conclusions and ramifications discussed are only relevant to North America. The principal outcome of the French-Indian War, from the British point of view, was that France had been nullified as an adversary in North America. To the casual observer of 1763, the situation at the end of the war presented Great Britain in undisputed control of North America east of the Mississippi River.

The situation quickly proved to be more complicated than first impressions indicated. Within a few months of the signing of the Treaty of Paris, a large-scale Indian insurrection had broken out. The British succeeded in quelling the revolt after a lengthy campaign, but the revolt raised several issues, relevant not only to relations with the Indians but also to ensure the security of new British territories. Great Britain's methods for dealing with both of these considerations only served to further alienate her subjects in the original Thirteen Colonies. Already aggrieved by numerous tensions that had arisen during the conduct of the war itself, the colonists were incensed by the government's use of armed troops to prevent their movements toward westward expansion and settlement.

The Thirteen Colonies did not feel it was their responsibility to help pay the costs of the war, and they had no intention of contributing funds for the upkeep of security along the frontier, which was widely considered to be there solely to obstruct the westward movement of settlers. The British government sought various ways of compelling the colonial governments to pay to support the Army's presence in North America, and debate on this and related issues raged between London and North America from 1764 until 1775. The colonists found the Quebec Act of 1774 to be particularly galling. In addition to making liberal provisions accommodating the language, religion, and laws of the French Canadian population, this act also gave the colony of Quebec administrative rights over the newly conquered territories of the Ohio River valley and extensive areas east of the Mississippi. Settlers in the Pennsylvania and Virginia regions were particularly incensed by this decision, as they had always claimed these regions as their own. (For more background on these issues, see Essential Histories, *The American Revolution 1774–1783*.)

The numerous grievances fermenting in the populations of the Thirteen Colonies had, by 1775, developed into open rebellion against the British Crown. The British Army had gained significant tactical expertise in fighting in North America during the French and Indian War, but by the time war broke out in 1775, many of the reforms instituted had been forgotten. The majority of senior officers in the British Army of this period had not waged war in North America; most of them had fought in Germany in the Seven Years' War. Those who had fought in North America were mostly contemptuous of the American soldiers' fighting capabilities, citing their experiences with provincial soldiers in the French-Indian War. In fact, the British officers disparaged the Americans' ability to wage a war as a unified entity, remembering, again, occasions during the French-War when colonial assemblies bickered and reneged on promises of supplies and men. In underestimating their colonial opponents, British leaders made a serious mistake, forgetting that the Americans had at their disposal a large group of veterans who had served in both the provincial and regular ranks. They were able to tap into a fund of knowledge and experience when the

Fort Detroit (Detroit Public Library)

fledgling United States set out to create a professional army in 1775.

France, to its credit, did not ignore the issues that had been responsible for her defeat in both the French-Indian and the larger Seven Years' War. The army implemented numerous tactical reforms. In fact, the army in North America had performed remarkably well, given the circumstances and constraints under which it was forced to operate. Many of the reforms were instituted in response to the French Army's poor performance in Germany. These reforms became the cornerstone of a movement that would lead eventually to successes for the French Army in the American Revolution (1778–83) and during the revolutionary and Napoleonic period. France was only too happy in 1778 to join the Thirteen Colonies in an open treaty, hoping to gain back some of the territories lost in the Seven Years' War. This strategy paid off to a certain extent; France did not regain New France in 1783, but she did regain some of her lost colonies in the Caribbean, and helped to inflict a defeat upon the British. Both of these achievements helped to restore morale within the French military establishment.

The expenses incurred in both the French-Indian War and the larger Seven Years' War put France in a difficult financial position. Her attempts at financial reform were not as extensive as her military reforms had been, and the construction of a new fleet, along with other military needs, strained the budget to breaking point in the 1760s. Successful involvement in the American Revolution brought more financial burdens but no new ways of releiving them. The French crown's mounting debt and attempts to get it under control are often cited as being among the principal causes of the French Revolution. In the end, a seemingly insignificant frontier campaign in a thinly settled colonial outpost was to have enormous long-term ramifications for two of Europe's greatest powers.

Further reading

Primary Sources:

Manuscript Sources:
British Library
Bouquet Papers
Haldimand Papers
Hardwicke Papers
Napier Papers
Newcastle Papers
Townshend Papers
Add 11813 Captain William Parry
    (RN) Louisbourg
Add Mss 45662 Journal of Richard Humphrys
Add Mss 15535 Plans of Military Operations
    in NA

Massachusetts Historical Society, Boston
Journal of Benjamin Dunning
Major John Hawks Orderly Books
Journal of David Holden
Diary of Timothy Nichols
Journal of David Sanders
James Wolfe's Journal (McGill University)

National Army Museum, London
7204-6-2 'Journal of unknown individual'
6707-1 Lt. T. Hamilton Journal
6807-131 Journal of Augustus Gordon
7803-18-1 Journal of Charles Lee
8001-30 Captain Phillip Townsend
6806-41 1st Marquis Townshend Papers
7311-85 Williamson Papers
6807-51 Orders given by Major General Wolfe

Public Records Office, London
Amherst Papers

Printed Sources:
'General Orders in Wolfe's Army' *Manuscripts
    Relating to the early History of Canada,*
    Quebec, 1875.
'Journal of Braddock's Campaign'
    JSAHQR, LVII.

'Journal of Beausejour' Sackville, N.B., 1937.
'Journal of the Expedition to the River St.
    Lawrence', London, 1760 (Sergeant- Major).
'Journal of the Siege of Oswego', *Military
    History of Great Britain, for 1756, 1757,*
    London, 1757.
*Naval and Military Memoirs of Great Britain
    1727–1783*, London, 1790.
The Northcliffe Collection, Ottawa, 1926.
'Reflections on the General Principles of War
    and on the Compositions and Characters
    of the Different Armies in Europe', *Annual
    Register*, 1766.
Amherst, J., *Journal of Jeffrey Amherst*,
    Toronto, 1931.
Amherst, W,. *Journal of William Amherst*,
    London, 1928.
Bradstreet, J., *Impartial Account of Lt Colonel
    Bradstreet's Expedition to Fort Frontenac*,
    London, 1759.
Brown, T., *A plain Narrativ of the uncommon
    Sufferings and Remarkable Deliverance of
    Thomas Brown*, Boston, 1760
Bougainville, L.A. de., *Adventure in the
    Wilderness*, Norman, Oklahoma, 1964.
Dalrymple, C., *Military Essay containing
    reflections of the raising, arming, clothing
    and Discipline of British Cavalry and
    Infantry*, London, 1761.
Doughty, A.G., (ed.) *The Siege of Quebec and
    the Battle of the Plains of Abraham* (6 Vols.),
    Quebec, 1901.
Dundas, Sir David, *Principles of Military
    Movement*, London, 1788.
Hamilton, C., (ed.) *Braddock's Defeat: Journal
    of Captain Robert Chomley's Batman;
    Journal of a British Officer; Halkett's Orderly
    Book*, Norman, Oklahoma, 1959.
King, T., *Narrative of Titus King*, Boston, 1938.
Knox, H. *Historical Journal of Campaigns in
    North America, 1757–1760* (3 Vols.),
    Toronto, 1914.
Loudon, J., *General Orders 1757*, New York, 1899.

Lowry, J., *A Journal of Captivity*, London, 1760.

Pargellis, S., (ed.) *Military Affairs in North America*, New York, 1936.

Pouchot, P., *Memoir of the Late War in North America between the French and the English*, Roxbury, Mass., 1864.

Quaiffe, M., (ed.) *The Siege of Detroit in 1763*, Chicago, 1958.

Rogers, R., *Journals of Major Robert Rogers*, Albany, 1883.

Sautai, M., (ed.) *Montcalm at the Battle of Fort Carillon*, Ticonderoga, N.Y., 1928.

Tomlinson, A., *Military Journals of Two Private Soldiers*, Poughkeepsie, New York, 1855.

Webb, T., *Military Treatise on the Appointments of the Army*, Philadelphia, 1759.

Wolfe, J., *Instructions to Young Officers*, London, 1768.

Yorke, P.C., (ed.) *Life and Correspondence of Phillip Yorke, Earl of Hardwick*, Cambridge, 1913.

Secondary Sources:

Anderson, F., *A People's Army: Massachusetts Soldiers and Society in the Seven Years' War*, Chapel Hill, North Carolina, 1984.

Anderson, F., *Crucible of War: The Seven Years' War and the Fate of Empire in British North America, 1754–1766*, New York, 2000.

Balisch, A., 'Infantry Battlefield Tactics in the 18th Century,' *Studies in History and Politics* 83–84.

Brumwell, S., *Redcoats: The British Soldier and War in the Americas, 1755–1763*, Cambridge, 2002.

Duffy, C., *The Military Experience in the Age of Reason*, London, 1987.

Eccels, W.J., *Essays on New France*, Toronto, 1987.

Fortescue, Sir John, *History of the British Army*, Vol. II, London, 1908.

Gipson, L.H., *The British Empire Before the American Revolution* (V–VIII), New York, 1936–1970.

Guy, A.J., *Economy and Discipline: Officership and Administration in the British Army, 1714–63*, Manchester, 1984.

Harper, J.R., *78th Fighting Fraser's in Canada*, Montreal, 1966

Houlding, J.A., *Fit for Service: Training of the British Army*, Oxford, 1981.

Hughes, B.O., *Open Fire: Artillery Tactics from Marlborough to Wellington*, Chichester, Sussex, 1983.

Kennett, L., *French Armies in the Seven Years War*, Durham, North Carolina, 1967.

Leach, D.E., *Arms for Empire: A Military History of the British Colonies in North America, 1607–1763*, New York, 1973.

Leach, D.E., *Roots of Conflict: British Armed Forces and Colonial Americans, 1677–1763*, Chapel Hill, North Carolina, 1986.

Middleton, R., *Bells of Victory: Pitt-Newcastle Ministry and conduct of the Seven Years' War*, Cambridge, 1985.

Nosworthy, B., *Anatomy of Victory: Battle Tactics 1689–1763*, Hippocrene, N.Y., 1992.

Pargellis, S., *Lord Loudon in North America*, New Haven, 1933.

Parkman, F., *Montcalm and Wolfe*, New York, 1995.

Richards, F., *The Black Watch at Ticonderoga and Major Duncan Campbell*, Glen Falls, NY, 1930

Riley, J., *The Seven Years War and the Old Regime in France: Economic and Financial Toll*, Princeton, New Jersey, 1986.

Schweizer, K., *England, Prussia and the Seven Years War: Studies in Alliance Policies and Diplomacy*, Lewiston, N.Y., 1989.

Stacey, C.P., *Quebec, 1759: The Siege and Battle*, Toronto, 1959.

Ultee, M. (ed.), *Adapting to Conditions: War and Society in the Eighteenth Century*, Alabama, 1986.

Unpublished Thesis:

Marston, Daniel 'Swift and Bold: The 60th Royal American Regiment and Warfare in North America, 1755–1765', M.A. Thesis, 1997, McGill University.

Index

Visit the Osprey website

- Information about forthcoming books

- Author information

- Read extracts and see sample pages

- Sign up for our free newsletters

- Competitions and prizes